The Punters' Guide to Democracy

Peter Emerson

The Punters' Guide to Democracy

What it is, Sadly; and What it Could be, Gladly

 Springer

Peter Emerson
The de Borda Institute
Belfast, UK

ISBN 978-3-031-06986-4   ISBN 978-3-031-06987-1   (eBook)
https://doi.org/10.1007/978-3-031-06987-1

This Springer imprint is published by the registered company Springer Nature Switzerland AG
The registered company address is: Gewerbestrasse 11, 6330 Cham, Switzerland

In Memoriam
Dr. John Robb
Founder and oft-time chair of the New Ireland Group

Foreword from Professor Katy Hayward

Although broadly taken to mean any member of the public, the term 'punter' properly refers to someone who has placed a bet or gambled on something. More generally, we might say, a punter is someone who has a stake of some sort in the outcome of an event or process. In this sense, *The Punter's Guide to Democracy* is precisely what we are in need of. For we all have a stake in the outcome of democratic processes—even those who choose not to exercise their right to vote. It is only right that we should know the bare essentials.

There are few people better qualified than Peter Emerson to write such a book. Good guides don't only point out and explain the important features of a subject, they also 'get under' its surface in such a way that stimulates the imagination. The very best guides can spark such a sense of revelation among punters that they cannot help but share what they have learned.

Peter Emerson has accomplished that in this little book. In some ways, his message is very simple: an electoral system (particularly a majoritarian one) does not a democracy make. But the context and the timing make this message seem all the more revelatory. Western liberal democracies facing exogenous and endogenous challenges that are potentially catastrophic if left unchecked, but elected governments are seemingly unwilling or unable to counter them. Our democratic processes do not disrupt such self-harming complacency; on the contrary, they largely perpetuate them.

We are already seeing the cracks in the edifice of our democracy. Emerson shows us that these cracks are not merely superficial but signs of a failure to have built our democratic processes and systems on much surer foundations.

We have chosen to embed an imbalance and an error in almost all our democratic processes, namely the assumption that, despite the nature of the human and natural world, complexity in decision-making is best avoided.

This book is written with wit and with a charming degree of respect for the intelligence and interest of the average punter. With the engaging fluency of a cultural polymath, Emerson draws knowledgeably upon the values and systems of different continents and generations. His technical explanations are rigorous but not laboured. And his argument for the common good is made not with any forlorn delusion but with a clear-eyed, crystal sharp assertion of what could be chosen to be done differently in order to achieve it.

'We deserve better' is the near-unavoidable conclusion for any reader. With this guide in hand, us punters are equipped to know how to make it so.

Belfast, UK   Katy Hayward
February 2022

Foreword from Professor 杨龙, Yáng Lóng

For years, people have been accustomed to see democracy as a majority decision, which is feasible in the case of a binary choice, but as long as more than two options exist, the binary voting system will suppress the minority or exclude a third option. In the process of a collective decision-making system, the problem of the binary voting system is more serious, because the policy alternatives are multiple in most cases, and the policy decided through the binary voting system will inevitably exclude some third choices, thus ignoring the interests or preferences of some persons.

In addition to telling us about the problems of the binary voting system, this book also generally introduces how to improve the decision-making voting system to solve the problems caused by binary voting. The method proposed by the author is to let all members who participate in the vote or decision-making to list their preferences according to the intensity of their preferences, and then select the fully accepted results after taking all preferences cast into account. This voting method can reflect the preferences of all members, and will not force anyone. The key to this approach is consensus through cooperation. To improve the efficiency of voting and improve the accuracy of preference expression, the author also introduces a method of preferential points, asking voters to score all preferences, then addition and calculation, the highest score preference becomes the collective decision.

This book presents good methods, and the next step is to design appropriate methods of decision voting based on different types of collective decisions or voting, so that they can be used by officials of all levels of institutions. Such improvements can make our public decisions fairer and reduce the conflicts of interest between persons.

Tiānjīn, China   杨龙 Yáng Lóng

Preface

The King is in the altogether, but all together, the altogether
He's altogether as naked as the day that he was born
And it's altogether too chilly a morn!

Car speedometers don't read just 'fast' or 'slow'; they're calibrated in kilometres per hour. Thermometers in ovens say more than 'high' or 'low'; they're measured in degrees. And life is full of precision instruments...

...except in politics. For in politics, we use the majority vote, a tool with only two readings: 'yes' and 'no'. Problems are complex. We all have preferences. But the instrument we use is almost always binary: 'for' or 'against', 'black' or 'white'—and not even one shade of 'grey' (let alone forty).

This blunt tool is ubiquitous, its use often iniquitous. It's in the United Nations Security Council where, to make matters worse, some countries have vetoes. It's probably in every elected chamber on the planet, from the United States Congress downwards... or should I say upwards. It was the very basis of the Soviet Union, where the term 'bolshevik' comes from the word '*bolshinstvo*' 'большинство' meaning 'majority'. It is used by the Chinese Communist Party Politburo Standing Committee, as for example in a crucial vote on Tiān'ānmén Square in 1989, (Sect. 6.4.2). It's in Article 97 of the

Constitution of North Korea, both simple and weighted. And it's used in political parties, trades unions, company boards, community associations and courts of law.

But this binary voting is primitive, often divisive, always Orwellian—'this' good, 'that' bad—sometimes hopelessly inaccurate, and at worst, a cause of violence. "All the wars in the former Yugoslavia started with a referendum," (*Oslobodjenje*, Sarajevo's legendary newspaper, 7.2.1999—Sect. 6.4.2), and the genocide in Rwanda began with the slogan, *"Rubanda nyamwinshi,"* 'we are the majority,' (Sects. 6.2.1 and 6.4.2).

Other voting instruments for identifying a 'democratic majority opinion' have long since been available; plurality voting for example, nearly 2,000 years old, was first used at governmental level about 1,000 years ago, in China (Sects. 6.2.2 and 6.3). What's more, some of the more modern procedures are precision instruments, calibrated not just with 'for' or 'against' but in preferences. The best of them, I argue, is a preference points system: it is robust, inclusive, and above all, accurate. And if it's more accurate than binary voting, then it is also more democratic. It was devised in 1770. All we have to do is (read on… and) use it.

The Book

It is odd, but many professional texts on democracy talk at great length about numerous and various electoral systems, with hardly a word about the several different voting systems for decision-making (Sect. 6.4.1). In like manner, politicians and activists in NGOs devoted to democratic reform often advocate preferential voting systems… in elections, yes… but say little or nothing about preferential voting systems in decision-making. Yet the way decisions are taken and/or ratified determines the very system of governance, and to a greater extent than the choice of electoral system.

Accordingly, this text concentrates on decision-making; there's a synopsis for all the busy professors and other professionals in Annex I, while the book itself is for the more patient punters. The first Chapter shows that binary voting is indeed blunt, very. It is also manipulable… and we all know that some politicians are manipulative… which partly explains why they like this binary voting. Chapter 2 describes some of the other decision-making voting procedures, a few of which are inclusive, accurate… sometimes disliked and often ignored. Next, Chap. 3 outlines the procedures for using a non-adversarial decision-making voting procedure—and this I feel is what should be the foundation of a truly democratic structure.

In fact, preferential voting fits into a holistic concept of democracy, if not indeed of life. Amongst its many virtues, the preferential points methodology is actually non-majoritarian—it can identify the option with the highest *average* preference, and an average, of course, includes *every* voter, not just a majority of them. So Chap. 4 shows how this methodology could well be the basis of a more inclusive democratic structure—all-party, power-sharing, coalition governments of national unity. Just to round things off, Chap. 5 does what many of those other political books do: it compares some of the world's electoral systems, but unlike many of those texts, it also describes what I think is the best system: a points preferential and proportional electoral system which could be the second corner stone of a consensual polity.

So far, the text has been pretty simple—it is, after all, the punters' guide—with only a few tables, no graphs at all, and no quotations, neither technical nor historical (except for one at the end of this Preface and two in Chap. 5). In what follows, however, the book becomes a little more academic, with references and so on... because this book is not just for the punters: it is also the professionals' guide, a handbook for politicians and decision-makers generally, for journalists and political scientists, and especially for students at both secondary and third levels. Then, looking back a little, Chap. 6 is a history of decision-making voting procedures, which is part of the history of the science of social choice—a subject that doesn't get anything like the attention it deserves. And looking forward, Chap. 7 talks of some of the many potentially beneficial consequences that might accrue if we can but persuade the world's politicians to use a form of decision-making which encourages, not confrontation, but cooperation.

Finally, the Epilogue. In brief, the book describes what democracy is but should not be, in Chap. 1; what it might be in Chap. 2; what and how it should be in Chaps. 3 and 4, {Chap. 5 is the little (but important) diversion into electoral systems}; how it came to be in Chap. 6, and what might be its benefits in Chap. 7. All that is left is in the Epilogue: the answer to the simple question—just what *is* democratic decision-making?

Now there are those who don't like this 'consensus nonsense' (as I have often heard it called), so there are a few annexes to explain some of the mathematical stuff. Annex I we mentioned is the synopsis. Annex II shows that binary voting can be not only capricious: at times it can be just crazy—a 'democratic' outcome can be literally anything at all! Annex III gets a bit technical and looks at single-peaked curves; it's well worth a glance, however, for it shows that a preferential points system can sometimes be not only extremely accurate, but also very difficult to manipulate.

Annex IV looks at partial voting and shows that, if the voting methodology uses the original Borda count BC formula {rather than the one which history has bequeathed—(Sect. 2.4)}, the voting procedure itself actually encourages all participants to vote and, in so doing, to cast all their preferences, i.e. to be truly democratic: literally everybody has a vested interest in voting; not just the majority, but also the minorities, all of them; everybody; we all like to influence the average.

The next one, Annex V, is all maths, and it gives the different consensus coefficient values involved in ballots of a different number of options. Annex VI shows what a matrix vote might look like in practice, in this instance as if in Germany. And finally, to sum up the entire book, Annex VII is a taxonomy of decision-making.

The Text

I refer to lots of unnamed persons—voters, chairpersons, Speakers, etc.—alternatively as male or female; indeed, in some instances, an individual may change from a he to a she and back again, with abandon; anything to keep the use of the rather cumbersome 'he/she' and 'his/her' combinations to a minimum.

Some authors use words for numbers less than ten, and digits for anything bigger. But I jump all over the place, in an effort—not vain I hope—to make everything more understandable.

I use the ordinals 1st and 2nd etc., to describe preferences, and occasionally results, while pretty well everything else is spelt out in full: first and second, etc. And one point of clarification: when talking about the matrix vote (in Chap. 4), I sometimes add up lots of points to get a 'sum', lots of sums to get a 'score', and lots of scores to get a 'total'.

That's it. In Hans Christian Andersen's fairy tale, a little boy is telling everyone the king is naked. Now, in these pages, this old boy is trying to say our democratic decision-making is also a sham, a dangerous sham. As Mikhail Gorbachev put it, "Not just the emperor but the entire 'court' [has] no clothes" (Gorbachev 1997: 264.). And politics will remain shambolic, the world will continue to suffer far too many 'chilly morns', for as long as the world's democrats, theocrats and autocrats think that decision-making is, and should be, or even must be, based on crude and crazy dichotomies.

Belfast, Northern Ireland   Peter Emerson
February 2022

Reference

Gorbachev, M. 1997, *Memoirs*, Bantam Books, London.

Acknowledgements

It's quite difficult to dissent, and it was ever thus. In some countries, of course, it was and is still much more difficult: you might get arrested, as in Russia—(I write these words on day fourteen of the 2022 Russian invasion of Ukraine)—imprisoned, tortured or even executed. Here in Northern Ireland, the Troubles now passed, the worst that can happen is that you just get ignored.

Some writers, like the palaeontologist Teilhard de Chardin, unpublished in his own lifetime, can work without encouragement. But not I. Fortunately, in one of those many coincidences which form a part of everyone's lives, I met Dervla Murphy, and she encouraged me to write, albeit not initially on voting but about my 1974 African adventures which, like hers, were by bicycle. *NE QUITTEZ PAS LA VOITURE!* ('Don't get out of your car!') said the notice at the entrance to the Virunga game park in Zaire (now DRC), all in bold black print. But there was no advice for the cyclist.

Dervla and I met in 1977 in Belfast, where I had 'settled' two years earlier. My English Catholic mummy was not too happy about this—Africa was fine, but the wild outback of Northern Ireland? The Troubles still raging? This was because, of course, she understood the problem: she had married an Irish Protestant. And maybe it is my mixed parentage which, more than anything else, prompted my career as a dissident. So first and foremost, my thanks go to mum and dad.

'Are you Protestant or Catholic?' the locals asked when I arrived. ("God knows," was my favourite response.). The question, of course, was always binary. 'Are you British or Irish?' was the other query. Basically, to be an Anglo-Irish agnostic was (and still is) beyond the parameters of 'normal' political dialogue. I nevertheless found a political home: the New Ireland Group NIG was founded in 1982 by the late John Robb—there aren't many of us left, nowadays—but I still get good support (and even better whiskeys) from Wes Holmes.

In 1985, you may remember, Britain and Ireland signed the (long overdue) Anglo-Irish Agreement. The Rev. (sic) Ian Paisley led a huge protest of 100,000 outside Belfast City Hall: 'Ulster says, "NO!" he screamed—as if the question was binary. So one week later, six of us stood at the same venue, in silence, with a banner which read, 'We have got to say 'yes' to something'. Just six individuals, Roy Garland also from the NIG, two Belfast Quakers and two others (whose names, alas, I forget), each giving the others encouragement.

The obvious follow-on, I thought, would be a public meeting, so that folks could indeed say 'yes' to something, if not *somethings*, to whatever constitutional arrangement(s) they liked: a 'yes' to their 1st preference, and perhaps also a 2nd preference 'yes' to their best compromise choice, and maybe some lower preference 'yeses' as well. But no 'noes'. I suggested this idea of a conference with preferential voting to Queen's University but... what? Republicans and Unionists in the same room? Far too dangerous! Their answer was another, though quieter, 'no'. Corrymeela, the peace organisation, was next, but they too declined. Not however the NIG. John was brilliant, his contacts in every sector of Irish society and especially here in the North were right and left across the board. Roy was also great, not least when we travelled to Portadown together, to persuade Ulster Clubs to join in. And Wes, our faithful secretary, never stopped.

May 1986. 'Will anyone come?' John asked when, well ahead of time, we arrived in Mandela Hall in Queen's Students' Union. One hour later, with over 200 sitting in a great big, tiered circle, we started. In silence. And the late John Hewitt read his poem, *The Anglo-Irish Accord*, specially written for the occasion.

THE ANGLO-IRISH ACCORD

These days the air is thick with bitter cries,
as baffled thousands dream they are betrayed,
stripped of the comfort of safe loyalties,
their ancient friends considered enemies,
alone among the nations and afraid.

And those who now most loudly mouth their fears
are webbed in spirals of rash verbiage
which, coarse with coloured epithets, appears
a rhetoric of cudgels, torches, spears,
loaded with vivid enmity and rage.

This land we stand on holds a history
so complicated, gashed with violence,
split by belief, by gallant pageantry,
that none can safely stir and still feel free
to voice his hope with any confidence.

Slave to and victim of this mirror hate,
surely there must be somewhere we could reach
a solid track across our quagmire state,
and on a neutral sod renew the old debate
which all may join without intemperate speech.

From *The Collected Poems of John Hewitt*,
ed. Frank Ormsby (Blackstaff Press, 1991),
reproduced by permission of Blackstaff Press
on behalf of the Estate of John Hewitt.

Thus the atmosphere was palpable.

(There were four more 'participants' at the entrance: two police officers on one side, huge fellers as they often are, just keeping their eyes on things; and opposite them, two 'wee hard men' from Sinn Féin, 'the boys', keeping their eyes on those eyes… *and* those things.)

Six hours later when the seminar of plenary sessions, workshops, breaks, debates, a multi-option vegetarian lunch and a multi-option preference vote, was all done, John said, 'Not yet have we learnt the significance of this day'. We still haven't.

That was the start of my dissent, and yes, I owe a huge debt of gratitude to John and the NIG. At the time, I knew nothing about voting theory, and nothing about other forms of multi-option decision-making.

'You'd better do some research', said Phil Kearney, (who also knew nothing about these voting procedures); he was and still is one of my colleagues in the Irish Green Party, which we and other dissenters of the ecological variety had helped to found in 1982. Another colleague, Professor John Baker of UCD, knew a lot, and he it was who first told me about the Condorcet rule, while another professor, Don Saari of the University of California introduced me to Duverger's Law. I was, after all, an unqualified dissident: a trained submariner, a retired maths and physics teacher, an experienced cyclist… but neither a psephologist nor a political scientist.

I joined the Society of Social Welfare and thus met some of the world's leading minds in voting theory—Maurice Salles, Hannu Nurmi and Don again, all of whom have been of great support—and by attending several conferences and organising a few of my own, I have also met many others, not least Don Horrowitz, the late Elizabeth Meehan, the late Sir Michael Dummett, Arend Lijphart, Iain McLean and Katy Hayward, professors all, and they too have given me every encouragement.

Initially, then, I knew little. It just seemed obvious, firstly, that in politics, binary voting is too primitive; secondly, that a preferential points system could perhaps be more inclusive. So I 'invented' a preferential points system of voting, only later to discover that it had already been invented… many times… not only now in Ireland but also, working backwards, in Brazil, Kiribati, England, France, Germany, and maybe too in Spain where it all started, in 1299.[1]

For various reasons, however, lots of people are convinced that, to be democratic, decisions should be taken in binary, majority votes. It is, if you like, an *idée fixe*—as if every political controversy has to be reduced to a dichotomy, or a series of dichotomies. In a nutshell, they say, a democracy should be majority rule—and I agree. The electoral system can be pretty well anything, they continue—I'm not so sure about that—but decisions in parliament should be taken in a majority vote—and here I definitely dissent. In a word, they believe in majoritarianism; I don't. They go on: if someone dissents from that belief, he/she is undemocratic or even anti-democratic. And they do go on. Hence, for instance, the reluctance of many in the media and academia to even discuss let alone question majoritarianism, and of many in the UK's Electoral Commission, for example, to even correspond. As far as the latter was concerned, to take a recent example, the vote on Brexit was binary, had to be binary, and couldn't be anything but binary.

---

[1] For decision-making, I (and others) devised the modified Borda count MBC; the quota Borda system QBS was Michael Dummett's invention; and the only voting procedure which I can claim to be all my own is the matrix vote.

But first, let's go back awhile. In the 1980s, I was campaigning—in every-thing but the crib, as they say in Belfast—I was talking about consensus voting to the Irish and British Greens, writing letters to the regional and national press, and using consensus decision-making with Rob Fairmichael and others at the peace camp at RAF Bishopscourt, our 1980s contribution to the 'ban the bomb' movement. Getting the Northern Ireland media to talk about consensus decision-making, however, was difficult. You might have thought that the above 1986 conference would have prompted a debate or two, but no. So, in desperation, I went to meet the BBC NI Controller, to ask for a programme on the subject. Oh we can't just do a programme; we have to have 'a hook', said he, on which to hang such a discussion.

In 1991, we held our fourth NIG cross-community consensus conference, on this occasion with electronic preference voting. Not bad for 1991. One of our guests was Michael D Higgins, the current President of Ireland—then 'only' a TD (MP) in the Irish Parliament, *Dáil Éireann*, but yet another of John's good contacts; another speaker was from Sarajevo, Petar Radji-Histić. Thus we tried to say, please, no binary referendums, not in Bosnia. Six months later in March 1992, Bosnia held the plebiscite… and, of course, imploded. So I went there, crossing the country, twice, in winter and in war, in order to say, on my return, that majoritarianism doesn't work there either. My mode of transport, as is my want, was the bicycle, mainly because, in war, it was safer that way. The journey took three months. Was the story good enough for a BBC-NI hook? No; they were not interested.[2] French national television, TFN1, yes; the *Irish News* yes; but BBC-NI said 'no'. (There are amazing stories of BBC and other journalists, risking their lives to bring us the truth, today in Ukraine, yesterday in Bosnia.) Why then did the local BBC-NI not report a local soul who was also working in a warzone? Was it because I might also talk of voting procedures? (It's not just BBC-NI, of course; the Green Party did not react at all, nor did the local universities; and for years, I have been trying to persuade the NI Community Relations Council, for instance, to look at the subject in more detail… in vain.)

Maybe the media would talk about my dissenting views when the method-ology had been adopted, or at least discussed, abroad. So in 1994, I wrote to BBC Radio 4, and while several journalists replied, John Humphrys and the like—their favourite word was 'interesting'—nothing ever happened. In 2012, I held a book launch in the House of Lords with the late Lord

---

[2] Campaigning for what were the then forthcoming council elections had not officially started, but I suspect one of the reasons for their disinterest was because they thought that any coverage for a candidate of the tiny little Green Party would be 'unfair' on 'the poor little' huge (Protestant extremist) Democratic Unionist Party, DUP.

Paddy Ashdown and Lord Mike Boyce, with the folk singer Tommy Sands in support—he has often introduced our consensus gatherings—but that too wasn't good enough for either Radio 4 or BBC-NI. Eventually, seven years later, when the binary business of Brexit was proving itself to be a total nonsense, I was at last invited to do two Radio 4 interviews, the second on their iconic *Today* programme.[3]

Several journalists have been great exceptions, of course. Joe Humphreys of the *Irish Times* played a magnificent role in a 2016 conference in Dublin on the matrix vote. Andy Pollak from the same stable often covered my work, especially when he was based up here in Northern Ireland. Likewise, Billy Graham in the *Irish News* always gave our NIG conferences extensive coverage, and in 1992, it was the then editor, Nick Garbutt, who gave me the necessary documentation to convert me into a journalist for my UN press pass for Bosnia.

Generally speaking, however, many in the media and the political science branch of academia don't like mathematics. The journalists might cover a conference, especially if they can get an interview with the Sinn Féin spokesperson…but voting systems, no. Maths doesn't sell newspapers, (unless it's on the horses).

Many politicians don't like sums either, (except when their own fates are at stake; oh yes, they love the polls). They call themselves democrats, of course. But democracy? Voting systems? Voting theory? Yet again, they say 'no', (and so too some of the pollsters). The politicians take majority votes, because that's the way to win, and to win everything, and secondly because that's the way everyone else does it. For most of them, democracy is win-or-lose. But happily quite a few others and not only I dissent.

At the founding convention of the Irish Greens in 1982, I gave a talk on consensus. We must live in sympathy with the environment, I argued, and the latter includes our neighbours; decisions should therefore depend neither on the force of arms nor upon the force of numbers. It then took us 12 months to sort out a common British/Irish/Northern Irish policy statement on the Troubles, and once that was done, we founded the Northern Ireland Green Party, and we again spoke of consensus. In effect, we were dissenting from the norm of NI politics, ecologically—that is, not only environmentally but also politically—and little surprise, therefore, that both in the media and in society at large, some regarded me as a bit of a crank. Today, happily, the circle has turned, and society now accepts that the Greens are a part of everyday politics. But unhappily—the *idée fixe* is so strong—the NIGP itself

---

[3] Maybe it would be more accurate to say, I invited them to invite me. *Today* did an outside broadcast from Belfast, so I had a little chat afterwards and…

is still using majority vote decision-making[4] and for a long time, some in the leadership have regarded this dissident as, well, a bit of a crank.

Not for this reason alone, but mainly because of yet more 'coincidences' (for which, I'm told, there is no word in Tibetan),[5] my campaigning has ventured abroad. In 1988, I moved to Moscow for a couple of years, wrote articles on consensus in *Moscow News* with my co-author, the late Irina Bazileva. And while I was there, I met a Georgian, then an ordinary punter, soon to be the Prime Minister of Georgia, the late Zurab Zhvania MP and, as a result, I gave a press conference (in Russian) in Tbilisi in 1990 on power sharing.[6] Since then, I have lectured in universities and institutes with Angela Mickley in Berlin, with Maurice (Salles) in Caen, Leo Joosten in Leiden, in Brussels with Jeremy Wates, in Brno care of Věra Stojarová, in Baku, Prague, Sarajevo, Sofia, Vienna, Warsaw and Yerevan, in Nairobi and Windhoek in Africa, in Canada and all across the States.

I now knew that this universal practice of binary voting was and is still a cause of much misery and mayhem, in almost every country in the world; not just in conflict zones like Northern Ireland, the Balkans, Rwanda, the Caucasus, Kenya, Ukraine and throughout the Middle East; not just in 'stable' democracies on both sides of the Atlantic and in Asia; but everywhere, including in one-party states, in the USSR as was, and in China. Accordingly, in 2017, I invited another host to invite me to be their guest, this time for a TEDx talk in Vienna. But instead of turning round and coming home again afterwards, I continued eastwards, overland, with my bicycle (now a fold-up—I'm getting old), to then give talks and so on in other universities and/or institutes, in Sarajevo care of Valery Perry, Tbilisi with Nato Kirvalidze, and Tehran with Ali Chaboki—my first lecture to an audience of chadors.

Turkmenistan doesn't like foreigners very much, so from Iran I flew to China, to Xīnjiāng, today's (but not yesterday's) home of the Uighurs and others; what with body searches and police patrols everywhere, Kashgar (Kāshí)was home from home for anyone who has lived through the Troubles in Belfast. Then it was back to surface travel, with over a dozen lectures on democracy in mainland China, and others in Hong Kong and Taiwan. As in Europe, so too in China, all of these talks could only be conducted with the support of colleagues, the likes of Professor Yáng Lóng 杨龙 in Nánkāi

---

[4] They often use the MBC (and not QBS) as an electoral system but not in decision-making, (even though the former is designed for decision-making, whereas QBS is the electoral system).

[5] The verb exists, one thing can indeed coincide with another. But to suggest the reason why is because of a coincidence is at best tautological.

[6] The British and Irish media were not interested, I'm afraid, neither in the publications nor in the press conference.

University, Professor Sòng Yīngfǎ 宋英法 in Xúzhōu, and (not a professor, not yet anyway) Fāng Yīng 方英 in Beijing.

Now you might think that the story of a 75-year-old learning some Chinese and then travelling overland from Belfast to Beijing and beyond—I got as far as Pyongyang—with lectures all over the place (though admittedly, none in North Korea), might get a mention on BBC NI. Quite a big hook, no? Wrong. Nothing. So I wrote another book on voting, my tenth. Still nothing. So I repeated the journey. On this occasion, I was detained by the Russian authorities when taking a minibus-taxi from Tbilisi to Vladikavkaz—they don't like NGOs very much either—but I still managed to give a lecture in Moscow University with Professor Fuad Aleskerov and Irina (Bazileva). I then took a second journey on the Trans-Siberian railway to give yet more lectures in China, this time with demonstrations of electronic preference voting—and yes, firewall or no firewall, university students in both Běijīng and Xúzhōu were able to download the de Borda soft-ware, no problem, *méi guānxi*, 没关系, as they say and write. Was the media interested? Ah ha! At last, the answer was 'yes'… but only because I was in there in February 2020 when, bingo—the Chinese word is 病毒 bìngdú—Covid. But voting, decision-making, no; they prefer to ignore that bit.

In all, then, I have managed to speak on democracy and stuff in universities in Africa, Asia, Europe and North America, and my latest achievement was a December 2021 zoom talk at a six-day, international conference on *Democracy—Shared Human Values*, hosted by the Chinese Academy of Social Science in Beijing. But I'm still not good enough for BBC NI, for example, or the NI Universities.

Yes, it is difficult to dissent. Now just because you dissent doesn't mean you are right, of course, to quote a Russian Orthodox cleric from Gorbachev's time. Happily, however, there are others who also persist in consistently insisting that pluralism is possible—some of the Greens like Phil (Kearney) and Vanessa Liston in Dublin with Mal O'Hara and Paul Veronica in Belfast, along with a few journalists as noted, and rather more academics, only some of whom I've mentioned. Yes, dissenters sometimes also go wrong, and if there are mistakes in the pages which follow, I'm the one to blame.

Overall, then, I must give a big thank you to all of my literate and/or numerate supporters. The first is indeed Dervla Murphy, definitely of the former category, who recently said preferential decision-making will one day have its Greta moment—Greta Thunberg—one day soon I hope, and only then will people wonder why the world used such a primitive tool as binary voting, even when other precision instruments were available. Next comes Phil, Elizabeth, Vanessa, Wes, Rob, Katy, Tommy, the two Johns—Robb and

Baker—and many others, who have helped me here in Ireland. While abroad, I am indebted to all sorts of contacts like the ones I have referred to above, many of whom have been my hosts on my umpteen travels.

In a nutshell, while lots of people don't, many others do believe in what I'm doing—not least my publisher. It is such a joy to have the backing of Johannes Glaeser and his colleagues in Heidelberg, who not only support but also trust me; as do my two foreword authors, Katy, another good cyclist (and, coincidentally, that was how we met), and Yáng Lóng, whose menu choices are the best in all China; as do my proof-readers, Alan Quilley a Quaker—no need to persuade him of the failings of majority voting—and for this volume, Rob (Fairmichael), the patient pacifist, who was also born onto a bicycle and into consensus, with John (Baker) helping out on Annex VII; and finally, as do others working in the background, like Martin who fixes my computer, Mark who maintains the de Borda website, and Davy who does my print-outs. *Go raith mile maith agaibh* to you all.

Belfast, UK   Peter Emerson
March 2022

Reviews

"…the West's relentless pursuit of binary voting… has been a cause of countless tragedies. This book is brilliant: political controversies should rarely if ever be 'resolved' by majority vote."
—Arend Lijphart, *Professor Emeritus of Political Science, University of California, San Diego*

"[for] those who do not believe in a black-or-white world… a very important and extremely timely contribution…"
—Věra Stojarová, *Associate Professor of Political Science, Masaryk University, Brno, Czech Republic*

"Peter's challenge to the binary "win-lose" approach is urgently necessary, as is his proposal for an eminently more reasonable, accountable, and participatory system."
—Dr. Valery Perry, *Democratization Policy Council, Sarajevo*

"…the preferential points vote… would be the more accurate way to make decisions, and the consequences far more peaceful."
—Lord Boyce, *House of Lords*

"He builds a case for a specific version of preferential procedure, not only for elections, but for decision making as well."
—Hannu Nurmi, *Professor Emeritus of Political Science University of Turku, Finland*

"A particularly strong plea in favour of voting procedures… which go far beyond the usual 'yes or no' ballots. [He uses] an alert prose and a wealth of illuminating and easily graspable examples."
—Maurice Salles, *Emeritus Professor, Université de Caen Normandie*

Contents

Abbreviations

AGM	Annual general meeting
AV	Alternative vote
BBC	British Broadcasting Corporation
BC	Borda count
BCE	Before the common era
CDU	Christian Democratic Union (*Christlich Demokratische Union*), (Germany)
DL	*Die Linke*, The Left, (Germany)
DPRK	Democratic People's Republic of Korea
DRC	Democratic Republic of Congo
DUP	Democratic Unionist Party
EC/EU	European Commission/Union
FDP	Free Democratic Party (*Freie Demokratische Partei*), (Germany)
FPTP	First-past-the-post
GNU	Government of National Unity
GOAT	Government of all the talents
GP	Green Party
IRV	Instant run-off voting
KGB (КГБ)	Комитет Государственной Безопасности, (Committee of State Security)
MBC	Modified Borda count
MMP	Multi-member proportional
MP	Member of parliament
NATO	North Atlantic Treaty Organisation
NGO	Non-governmental organisation

NI	Northern Ireland
NIG	New Ireland Group
NIGP	Northern Ireland Green Party
NZ	New Zealand
OSCE	Organisation for Security and Cooperation in Europe
PNG	Papua New Guinea
PR	Proportional representation
PV	Preference voting
QBS	Quota Borda system
RAF	Royal Air Force
RCV	Ranked choice voting
SNP	Scottish National Party
SPD	Social Democratic Party (*Sozialdemokratische Partei Deutschlands*), (Germany)
STV	Single transferable vote
TD	*Teachta Dála* (member of *Dáil Éireann*, the Irish Parliament)
TEDx	Technology, Entertainment, Design (x = independent)
TRS	Two-round system
UCD	University College Dublin
UK	United Kingdom
UN	United Nations
USA	United States of America
USSR	Union of Soviet Socialist Republics

List of Figures

List of Graphs

List of Tables

1

AI, Artificial Incompetence—The Ubiquitous Use of Binary Voting

Hippodamus "has a not unreasonable dissatisfaction with the simple 'yes or no' verdicts…"

Aristotle, *The Politics, II viii.*

Abstract Binary voting is one way of making decisions, but it is probably the crudest voting procedure ever devised. It has many failings, one of the biggest of which lies in the fact that it is often inaccurate; secondly, it's so easy to manipulate. Little wonder then that, in many instances, that which is declared to be the 'democratic will' is perhaps the will of only its author, and not necessarily the will of parliament let alone 'the will of the people'.

Keywords Majority voting · Manipulation · Win-or-lose · Adversarial politics · Democratic majority opinion

1.1 Introduction

Life is full of questions, from 'What's for lunch?' to 'How do we tackle Climate Change?'.

We start with the first one. Let's imagine a group of 14 people choosing a vegetable for the main course. The garden is not full, and the choice is limited to just four options: *A* artichokes, *B* broccoli, *C* cabbage or *D* dill. Maybe the democratic thing to do is to take a vote. 'Who wants *A*?' someone asks, but only 5 vote in favour and 9 vote 'no'. So, a majority doesn't want *A*; the democratic will of the 14 is 'no artichokes'. And that's that!

© The Author(s), under exclusive license to Springer Nature Switzerland AG 2022
P. Emerson, *The Punters' Guide to Democracy*,
https://doi.org/10.1007/978-3-031-06987-1_1

OK, next question, 'Who wants **B**?' And **B** loses by 4–10. So the democratic will is now 'no broccoli either'. That's another that. It gets worse. **C** is opposed by 11 and **D** by a dozen.

The will of the 14, therefore, is that they don't want **A** or **B** or **C** or **D**. But they don't want nothing either; they're hungry.

Maybe a different type of binary voting would be better, not a question of the 'Option **X**, yes or no?' variety like the one we've just been using, but an enquiry which poses an alternative: 'Option **X** or option **Y**?'

Well, with four options, there are quite a few pairs or pairings as they are called: 'Would you prefer **A** to **B**?' or '**A** to **C**?' or '**A** to **D**?' And there are three other pairs: **B/C**, **B/D** and **C/D**, six in all. Now as we've just seen, **A**, **B**, **C** and **D** are supported by 5, 4, 3 and 2 persons, respectively. So **A** is more popular than **B** by 5:4, and this we write as **A** > **B**. **A** also beats **C** by 5:3 and **D** by 5:2. Next we see that **B** > **C** by 4:3 and **B** > **D** by 4:2. And finally, **C** > **D** by 3:2. That's another load of thats.

To summarise it all, when we use an 'Option **X**, yes or no?' type of binary question, the answer is nothing; and when we use 'Option **X** or option **Y**?"'comparisons, the answer is anything; well almost anything: it can be **A** or **B** or **C**. In a nutshell, in some settings of binary voting, the answer depends entirely upon the question.

In other words, majority voting is manipulable and, as we recognised in the preface, some politicians are manipulative. Indeed, history is full of manipulations in which majority voting has been the decision-making voting procedure of choice, many leading to bitterly cold 'chilly morns'. We can mention a few dictators, starting with Napoléon Bonaparte who most certainly didn't like this 'consensus nonsense' and, in 1803, he used a majority vote referendum to become the emperor. Others include Vladimir Ilyich Lenin, who in 1902, as implied in the preface, thus set up his Bolsheviks; Adolf Hitler, who become the führer in this way in 1936 (both in para 6.4.2); and Saddam Hussein who in 2002 was re-elected president, supposedly with 100% support on again supposedly a turnout of 100%. All these votes were binary, all supposedly democratic and all were successful, of course—for the authors! Indeed, there has been only one dictator who, with regard to majority voting, 'couldn't dictate properly', and that was Augusto Pinochet: in 1988 he lost his third referendum by 57–43%.[1] We should also mention that the first dictator to get 100% was an Irishman: Bernardo O'Higgins scored a century to become *El Supremo* in Chile in 1818. When Napoléon became

---

[1] Another dictator also lost—Robert Mugabe in the year 2000, 45–55%—but prior to his referendum, he had dictated that it would be non-binding... so he actually lost nothing.

Table 1.1 A voters' profile

Preferences	Number of voters and their preferences			
	5	4	3	2
1st	*A*	*B*	*C*	*D*
2nd	*D*	*D*	*D*	*C*
3rd	*C*	*C*	*B*	*B*
4th	*B*	*A*	*A*	*A*

Emperor—a bit of an amateur really—he got only 99.7%—in like manner, Saddam Hussein on his first attempt at the presidency in 1995 scored a paltry 99.99%.

It's not only the 'democratic dictators' who like binary ballots, of course, for many 'dictatorial democrats' do the same. And usually, they too get what they want, because as often as not, they too set the question—just like he who asks, 'D'you want me to be emperor?' they sometimes ask, 'D'you want this bit of land to be independent?' or 'Do you want "this" (or these) policy/ies² rather than "that" (or those)?' on topics ranging from prohibition to electoral reform—and the question is, usually, the answer.

1.2   The Binary Ballot

OK, binary voting is not very good, so let us try to be a little more sophisticated. Let us ask the 14 hungry voters for their more nuanced opinions, and let's assume they have the preferences shown in Table 1.1.

Umm, it seems that opinions on artichokes are very divided: 5 think they are the best, but 9 regard them as the worst! Opinions on *B* are also rather polarised. So maybe *C* or *D* would be the most acceptable choice and... oh look, while option *D* has only a couple of 1st preferences, it is the 2nd preference of everybody else! So obviously *D*, dill, best represents the collective choice, everyone's best possible compromise.

But what happens if these 14 folks resort to a vote? Well, as we've just seen, if they use 'Option *X*, yes or no?' type questions, the answer is nothing; and when they use the 'Option *X* or option *Y*?' type of ballot, the answer—*A*, *B* or *C*—is anything but the right answer! So yes, majority voting is totally inappropriate in such a multi-option setting. With binary voting, the politician or chef who doesn't want *D* can just cook the books by choosing the

---

² In 2007, Hugo Chávez asked the people of Venezuela 36 questions, all to be answered in just one 'yes' or 'no'. He lost all of them, by 49.4–50.6%.

two options necessary for him to get the outcome she wants… and she then pretends this is the collective will.[3] If we use a multi-option voting procedure, however, we might get a more accurate result; this we will try to do in Chap. 2… and succeed in doing in Chap. 3. For the moment, however, let's take a closer look at this practice of binary voting.

1.3   Majority Rule

Now many people think that, in theory, democracy is the opposite of minority rule… which is true. Therefore, they assume, democracy must be majority rule. The former, minority rule is bad; so the opposite, majority rule must be good. (All very binary, so far, but nevertheless, so far so good.)

Unfortunately, many then make the huge mistake of thinking that a majority opinion can be identified by a majority vote, which is not true. This is not least because the 'majority opinion'—'Napoléon to be the emperor', 'Scotland/Croatia/Timor-Leste/Donetsk, to be independent', 'the UK to leave the EU', whatever—has to be identified earlier if it is to be already on the ballot paper. At best, a majority vote *might* be able to *ratify* something, if by accident or design the author has managed to spell out this collective will as an option… but it cannot *identify* anything, if, that is, the debate consists of more than two options.[4]

In a nutshell, we need a democratic procedure by which, firstly, the people or their representatives choose the options; only then perhaps can they all vote. But let us start with the theory. Now in any multi-option debate, as with our 14 lunch-goers:

> when there is no majority *in favour* of any one option, then, obviously, there is a majority *against* every option.

---

[3] In effect, this is what Boris Johnson did in the British House of Commons in 2020 on Brexit. He decided—dictated—that 'his deal' would be the option *X*, and that 'no deal' would be the option *Y*. All the other possibilities he just ignored.

Amazingly, lots of people in the media and academia regarded this decision as democratic. But this little old boy said nonsense. What's more, I had predicted it would be nonsense. In February 2016, four months *before* the UK's wretched Brexit referendum, I'd issued a press release to warn that any binary ballot would get a negative response. Accordingly, in its stead, I'd recommended a multi-option vote.

[4] Scotland, for example, could become the third member of a W-I-S-E—Wales, Ireland, Scotland, England—Federation… but only if such an option is on the ballot paper, along with other equally valid options; a short list of up to six options is probably advisable.

This truism (or something similar) was presumably known to the Ancient Greeks who realised that, if and when there are more than two options on the table—in other words, in politics, almost always (para 2.1)—then there has to be some sort of structure (para 6.2.3). Otherwise, as we've just seen, the outcome of any process based on binary voting—and in those days of your yore, majority voting was the only decision-making voting procedure known—could be almost anything, **A** or **B** or **C**. Indeed, with some voters' profiles like ours in Table 1.1, binary voting is guaranteed to be wrong!

1.3.1 The Old Days

So—back to the Greeks—they devised a set of rules. During the last 2,500 years, scientists and others have invented lots of amazing machines, from bicycles to computers, but when it comes to decision-making, we are all still using this ancient binary methodology under those ancient rules … and it works like this. If someone has moved a motion and others have suggested amendments, the procedure is as follows:

- first, identify the more/most popular amendment;
- next, accept or reject this favoured amendment, to get what we call the substantive;
- finally, choose between this substantive and the status quo.

Accordingly, in a very simple scenario of one motion and two amendments, everything shall be decided with just three binary votes, as shown in Fig. 1.1.

So let's consider the simplest of all settings, the minimum pluralist society, a committee of three persons with three different points of view, as shown in Table 1.2. They're still debating the question of lunch; the chef put dill on the menu, but none of the three like dill very much. Ms i moves a motion, 'Let's have artichokes instead'. Option **A**. Mr j proposes the first amendment in good democratic style: 'delete the word "artichokes" and insert "broccoli"'— and if adopted, this would become option **B**. Ms k prefers cabbage, option **C**. And let's assume they have the preferences as shown in Table 1.2.

Fig. 1.1 A 'Democratic' debate

Table 1.2 The threesome

Preferences	Ms *i*	Mr *j*	Ms *k*
1st	*A*	*B*	*C*
2nd	*B*	*C*	*D*
3rd	*C*	*D*	*A*
4th	*D*	*A*	*B*

$$
\begin{array}{c}
B \\
v \quad = \quad \dots \\
C \qquad v \quad = \quad \dots \\
A \qquad v \quad = \quad \dots \\
D
\end{array}
$$

Fig. 1.1a The first democratic debate—procedure

$$
\begin{array}{c}
B \\
v \quad = \quad B \\
C \qquad v \quad = \quad A \\
A \qquad v \quad = \quad D \\
D
\end{array}
$$

Fig. 1.1b The first democratic debate—result

The procedure, as depicted in Fig. 1.1a, involves three binary votes.

Now looking at Table 1.2, we see that *A* is more popular than *B* (by 2 votes to 1), which we write as *A* > *B*; we also see that *B* > *C*, that *C* > *D* and that *D* > *A*, (again, all by 2 votes to 1). So the outcome to the first ballot—the choice of the more preferred amendment, *B* or *C*—is a win for *B*; in the second ballot, *B v A*, the answer is *A*, which therefore becomes the substantive; and the final ballot, *A v D*, is a victory for *D*, as in Fig. 1.1b.

So democratically, this committee of three, who agree, unanimously, that *they don't like dill,* decide by a majority of 67% that *they like dill*. The answer is wrong. Good heavens! So binary voting, sometimes, can be inaccurate.

1.3.2   The Binary Paradox

Looking at those pairings, I suppose we could try to see which one is most popular by putting them all in order. Well *A* > *B* and *B* > *C*, so *A* > *B* > *C*. Next? Well *C* > *D*, so *A* > *B* > *C* > *D*. And *D* > *A*. So that means *A* > *B* > *C* > *D* > *A*... and, oh dear, it goes round and round in circles, forever. Amen. The paradox of binary voting, as it's called. It basically means, whenever there is a paradox, that no matter what the outcome (of whatever dubious process some devious politician has concocted), there will always be a majority that wants something else. In other words, majority voting may not be the best way of resolving a dispute; indeed, in many circumstances, such binary ballots have exacerbated tensions in societies, as in Northern Ireland, the Balkans, the Caucasus, Ukraine and so on.

In a three-option debate, you can indeed, sometimes, get a paradox. When there are four options, you might get a paradox amongst just three options or even, as in our current example, with all four options. Yes, $A > B > C > D > A$, and the other two pairings for those options which aren't adjacent to each other, are $C > A$ and $B > D$.

So now let's see just how frail any binary procedure can be. Adopting the procedure outlined above in Fig. 1.1, with all three members always voting in accordance with their preferences as shown in Table 1.2, let's see what happens if Mr j dominates the discussion and gets his 1st preference, B, as the motion, in which case options A and C are amendments. OK, round one, $A \, v \, C$, and the more preferred amendment is C. Next is $C \, v \, B$, so the substantive is now B. And finally, $B \, v \, D$, and the outcome is B, all terribly democratic, as shown in Fig. 1.2. Again by 67%. You can't argue against that, can you? Except that it's different from what we got in Fig. 1.1b.

The conclusion is pretty horrible: if you can't manipulate the question, you manipulate the debate.

Or again, if Ms k manages to manipulate things, if the motion is for cabbage and so A and B are the amendments, it's $A \, v \, B$ to give A; next, $A \, v \, C$ to give C; and finally, $C \, v \, D$ to give another, oh very democratic outcome, option C (Fig. 1.5).

$$
\begin{array}{ccccccc}
A & & & & & & \\
v & = & C & & & & \\
C & & v & = & B & & \\
 & & B & & v & = & B \\
 & & & & D & &
\end{array}
$$

Fig. 1.2 The second democratic debate—result

$$
\begin{array}{ccccccc}
A & & & & & & \\
v & = & A & & & & \\
B & & v & = & C & & \\
 & & C & & v & = & C \\
 & & & & D & &
\end{array}
$$

Fig. 1.3 A third democratic debate—result

In summary, binary voting is such a blunt tool, anything and everything is possible. Furthermore, if the chef's menu does not offer dill but one of the other vegetables, while the other three take it in turn to propose the motion or one of the two amendments, the 'democratic will' of the committee could be literally anything at all... as shown in Annex II.

1.3.3   The Blunt Instrument

Binary voting is indeed manipulable. It gets worse. As we've just seen, if the chair knows the voters' preferences constitute a paradox, she may arrange the debate to produce whatever result she wants. Worst of all, however, is this. If there is no paradox, if there is actually a majority in favour of something which she herself does not want, she can simply add another vegetable to the debate—'Hang on everyone, (after all, I am the chair), what about endives, option E?' or 'fresh peas, grape leaves... F, G...'—just as many options as are required to split that majority... after which, she can adjust the debate, as she wants, to get the outcome she wants. It's another form of divide and rule. And it explains why, in binary politics, the role of chair can be of overriding importance.

In all, binary voting is inadequate, inaccurate, and for all matters modern and controversial, totally inappropriate. It's OK if the subject matter is quite uncontentious—questions such as, 'Shall we now break for coffee?' 'Shall we celebrate the chair's birthday?'—can easily be resolved by a show of hands and a majority in favour. If, however, the topic is divisive and/or if a fair number of people object, using a majority vote as a peaceful means of dispute or conflict resolution should never even be contemplated! Not in a democracy, not ever.

1.4   The Binary Debate

Political debates are often pretty ugly, with those involved sometimes hurling abuse at each other in a spectacle of unruly behaviour; indeed, as often as not, the consequences of using a binary vote as the final deciding factor can be several.

Initially, in any debate on any contentious topic, there may well be lots of options 'on the table'. If the process might end in a majority vote, however, once the discussions start, some of these options might be pushed off; the temperature can rise; the arguments perhaps become heated... until it all boils down to just two, supposedly mutually exclusive opposites.

A chair might try to placate things and, in so doing, return to the original motion… but that means that some debates go round in circles.

Thirdly, there may even be such a thing as a 'wrecking amendment', an amendment which, if accepted and incorporated into the original motion, makes the latter contradict itself.

Fourthly, binary voting may divide a society as yet undivided, or exacerbate the divisions of a plural society. What's more, the debate may well deteriorate into an argument between two extremes, and those options which are pushed off the table are often the more moderate ones. To put it simply, in any 'X or Y?' ballot, the X supporters will not warm to any variation on the X theme. And in real life, X supporters often show more dislike of any X' variation than they do of the supposed opposite, option Y. As the old saying goes, 'the best is the enemy of the good', and the same applies to the 'worst' and the 'bad'—hence the paramilitary feuds which have afflicted so many conflicts.

Indeed, in a divided society, the most extreme variety on one side of the divide actually benefits from their opponents, without whom they could not be so negative. The extremist Unionist/Nationalist/Serb/Croat/Hutu/etc. often opposes the moderate. Furthermore, the former wants any contest to be just binary—extremists, almost by definition, want to win, and to win everything; 'compromise' for them is a dirty word. Not for them this 'consensus nonsense'.

And lastly, the outcome of any binary vote may sometimes be pretty meaningless. In 1999, many a referendum question could have been posed in Kosova—'Independence, yes or no?' 'Integration with Albania?' 'A Greater State with Albania, Kosova and Tetovo?'[5] Doubtless, any one of those questions would have received a level of support well in excess of 90%, and doubtless too the Kosovo Serbs would have boycotted such a poll… as did the Catholics in Northern Ireland in 1973, the Orthodox in Croatia in '91, the Cree Indians in Quebec in 1995, the Tatars in Crimea in 2014, and so on… ad nauseam. So even Stalinist-type majorities of 99%, as in Northern Ireland in '73, Kosova in '91, Bosnia in '92, can mean little, let alone majorities of <1% as in Quebec in '95, Uruguay in '96 and Wales in '97, to list just three of them; there have been at least 45 such 1% referendums since the first tight contest in 1866, and quite a few equally close parliamentary votes, everywhere.[6]

---

[5] Tetovo is the western province of North Macedonia.
[6] See Footnote 6 of para 7.3 for the 'won by one' webpage.

1.4.1 The Belfast Agreement

Most binary ballots offer a 'choice' of only two (extreme) alternatives. In divided societies, as we've just noted, binary voting often exacerbates those divisions, while in 'normal' societies, it can be the catalyst of populism. Admittedly, there is always the possibility that the members of parliament, or the people in a referendum, may be presented with a compromise, and such was the case in Northern Ireland (not in 1973 at the time of the Border Poll but) in 1998 with the referendum: 'The Peace Agreement, yes or no?' And the answer was 'yes'—brilliant. It was nevertheless all top-down politics. Some of the very people who had been part of the problem chose a solution which suited them, and the people were entitled to say only 'yeah' or 'nay'. Happily, the answer was in favour. That's not to say, however, that a more inclusive agreement might not have been even more popular.

One major faultline in that Agreement lays in its failure to consider other than binary voting in decision-making. At some stage in the future, Northern Ireland will have a referendum on whether or not to change its constitutional status and, as it stands at the moment, the question will be binary. Now if two people want to live together, then, of course, they may, but according to the law, both must consent. In contrast, if two communities are to live together, then, according to the Belfast Agreement, consent requires only the say of the bigger one. This is bizarre if not downright dangerous. In theory, when it's 50/50, everything could change if and when one Catholic individual reaches their 18th birthday and becomes eligible to vote. 50% + 1, that's democracy, some say. A united Ireland. Unless, the day before the vote, someone kills two of the other side... any two will do... 50% − 1... so NI stays in the UK (for another seven years anyway).[7] It's called a Peace Agreement.

Decision-making in the Assembly is also binary, albeit under the rules for twin majorities. Basically, if the Unionists say 'yes' and the Nationalist say 'yes', then 'yes' it is. The trouble is, of course, that one side or the other then has the power of veto, and if one side does say 'no', then it's impasse. The second bigger trouble is that, prior to the vote, everyone has to know who is what—Unionist, Nationalist or 'other'—and thus the Peace Agreement perpetuates the very sectarianism that it was supposed to overcome (para 7.2.1).

---

[7] The Belfast Agreement caters for a referendum—or a "never-end-'em"—every seven years or so, if the answer is 'no'. If it's 'yes', that's it, no re-plays, it's a united Ireland (of one sort or another), supposedly for ever.

1.4.2 Stable Democracies

Binary voting is dreadful from so many points of view. It's pretty bad in so-called 'stable' democracies where at worst, as in the USA, which probably have the most binary political structure on the planet, it is a major cause of a dysfunctional polity. They have a binary electoral system, first-past-the-post FPTP,[8] and possibly the world's most binary of all-party structures, its two-party system. And Donald Trump was only the (almost) inevitable consequence of binary politics, not just in their electoral system but, worst of all, in their addiction to binary voting in Congress.

1.4.3 Ethno-Religious Conflicts

Needless to say, in conflict zones, binary voting is often a major part of the problem. In any two-sided debate—"Are you Catholic or Protestant?" (Northern Ireland), "Sunni or Shi'a?" (Yemen), "Serb or Croat, Orthodox or Catholic?" (Croatia), "French or English-speaking?" (Quebec), "Hutu or Tutsi?" (Rwanda)—binary voting can be divisive. Not only that; almost by definition, this exclusive procedure can exclude (if not, in effect, disenfranchise) any voters who are partners in or the adult children of a mixed relationship, let alone any who might otherwise want to vote for a compromise. In brief, you cannot best achieve peace and reconciliation by using a voting procedure which is inherently divisive. Shouldn't that be obvious?

1.5 Conclusion

Binary voting, by definition, is exclusive. Everything is win-or-lose. The winners are included, totally; and the losers are excluded, equally totally. Democracy, however, is meant to be for everybody—it's meant to identify the *common* good. Politics, they say, is the art of compromise. But in many votes—divisions as they are called in some parliaments—there is no commonality, no compromise is on offer. The question is indeed blunt: it's 'this' or 'that', 'black' or 'white', 'left-wing' or 'right', and there aren't any other options on the ballot paper. There is no grey, no middle ground, and no compromise.

In a nutshell, binary voting in the elected chamber is a recipe for dysfunction. In many instances, therefore, binary voting promotes *artificial*

---

[8] Otherwise known as 'Fake-Post-Truth-Polling'… but not by Mr. Trump.

incompetence or faulty decision-making. The use of such a primitive instrument all but guarantees that the outcome will sometimes be wrong. Worse still, in conflict zones, it can and often does provoke violence.

There is a better way, a more scientific way. We humans are perfectly capable of having rational, multi-option debates; and we can best do so if these discussions include the possibility that all may participate in choosing the options, and conclude, if conclude they must in a vote, with a voting procedure which allows all these participants to retain their rationality. That means the voting instrument should be calibrated, a measure not just of two options, 'for' and 'against', but one which has several readings... called preferences. We need a voting procedure which allows us to relish our natural human diversity. It's time to turn the page.

Reference

Aristotle. (1992). *The politics*. London: Penguin.

2

Oh Lord, Give Me Consensus, But Not Yet—Pluralism is Possible

Asking yes-or-no questions is very unAfrican.
Hon. Senator Ephrem Kanyarukiga*
Formerly of the Adventis University of Central Africa,
currently a member of the Upper Chamber in Rwanda's Parliament.

Abstract There are quite a few voting procedures which can be used to identify a democratic majority opinion. They range from the blatantly inappropriate binary methodologies, via several more exact ones, to a few which are robust, inclusive, accurate and *very* democratic. And while majority voting provokes division, a preferential points system of decision-making can promote rational discourse and sound decisions; it can be, in effect, the very catalyst of consensus.

Keywords Consensus · Compromise · Democratic majority opinion · Democratic decision-making · Pluralism · Modified Borda count (MBC) · Consensus voting

---

*Hon. Senator Ephrem Kanyarukiga—A member of the audience at a press conference in Kigali on 6th March 2003, which I also attended. It was hosted by the Rwandan Government's National Unity and Reconciliation Commission to launch its report, "Participation in Gacaca and National Reconciliation." The 'gacaca courts' were established in 2001, mini 'peace and reconciliation commissions', to investigate the 1994 genocide (see also paras 6.2.1 and 6.4.2).

© The Author(s), under exclusive license to Springer Nature Switzerland AG 2022
P. Emerson, *The Punters' Guide to Democracy*,
https://doi.org/10.1007/978-3-031-06987-1_2

2.1   Introduction

Politicians often use the word 'consensus'—it falls into the 'sunshine' and 'apple pie' category—but they continue to use a binary voting procedure. There is even the bizarre contradiction that certain US presidents like Barack Obama and Joe Biden—(but certainly not the guy who came in between)—often call for bipartisan politics… yet do not consider reforming the decision-making voting system used in Congress, the wretched partisan binary vote. The latter measures, not the degree of *consent* but, the very opposite, the level of *dissent*. Sadly, many politicians fail to recognise that the word 'consensus' does not mean 'unanimity'. Nor are they aware that the sophisticated preferential points voting procedure can not only *identify* a consensus opinion—if and when there is a consensus, as it were waiting to be identified—it can actually measure the *degree* of consensus.

But we start at the beginning. In modern pluralist societies, no controversy is binary. Not, that is, if the society is pluralist. Not, that is, if it's democratic. (Almost) nothing. And therefore, as we said in Chap. 1, no controversy should be resolved by a binary vote. Well maybe there is one political question which is in fact binary: 'Which side of the road shall we drive on?' It has often been asked, and one country actually held a referendum on the subject: Sweden in 1955. And believe it or not, there were not two but three options on the ballot paper: 'left', 'right' and 'blank'. Lots of people wanted the first option; others preferred the second; while a third category were actually indifferent. Society had nevertheless decreed that the matter would be resolved in a ballot and, as committed democrats, they too wanted to play their part… and this they could do by voting 'blank' to thus, as it were, go with the (traffic) flow. It was November. It was not hot. Yet some 40,000 Swedes put on their boots, went to the polling stations, and voted 'blank'.[1]

So even if there was a political choice which was actually binary, there might still be more than two ways of voting.

2.1.1   The Wrong Question

But let us step back a moment. If a question is in fact binary, well, maybe it should have been posed differently. 'Shall we have broccoli for lunch dear, yes or no?' could perhaps be better phrased as, 'What shall we have for lunch?' Let the question be open. 'Dear'.

---

[1] 83% said 'left', 15.5% wanted 'right' and 1.6% voted 'blank'. The government however ignored everything, and Sweden now drives on the right.

Likewise in politics. Questions such as 'Capital punishment, yes or no?' should best be replaced by something like, 'How shall society deal with the convicted murderer?' In such an instance, the debate preceding the vote might be less emotive and more rational; it might even consider options like restorative justice. Or take the budget: it does not have to be, 'The ruling party's proposal, yes or no?' Maybe another party has an alternative budget. Maybe all of them have. Maybe the matter should be resolved in a multi-option vote.

Other binary questions should never even be asked: 'Are you Protestant or Sunni or Serb or French-speaking or Hutu?' and so on, (para 1.4.3). Likewise the question, 'Are you communist or capitalist?'—the dichotomy that led to the Cold War and, very nearly, the end of humankind. Just as the Protestant and Catholic are both Christian, and the Sunni and Shi'a both Muslim, and the Hutu and Tutsi both Rwandan, so too the communist and capitalist had much in common: they were both ideologies (if that's the right word) based on the exploitation of nature—each a creed of greed.

2.2 The Democratic Majority Opinion

We'll take a look at the history of voting in Chap. 6; at this stage, we need only repeat the fact that minority rule is wrong and that its opposite, majority rule, is a no-brainer (para 1.3). The question, then, is how best can we identify a democratic majority opinion?

Well, as we've just seen, we can't do it if some executive has given its parliament, or some parliament has given the people, just a binary choice: 'Do you want our 1st preference or our 2nd preference?' Or maybe the question was just a Napoleonic 'My 1st preference, yes or no?' We could perhaps hold a fair—or at least fairer—binary vote, if a citizens' assembly or public enquiry first looked at the problem to then recommend what should be on the ballot paper; it would be even better, of course, if such an impartial body produced a short-list choice of about five options.[2] It could also be done in a citizens' initiative, perhaps, but while over the years quite a few referendums in a fair number of countries have been multi-optional—the first was a three-option plebiscite in New Zealand in 1894—citizens' initiatives have invariably been binary.

---

[2] This is what happened in New Zealand, in 1992, much to the chagrin of the political parties. An independent enquiry produced a multi-option referendum offering everyone a choice of five different electoral systems (para 3.2.1, Footnote 3).

Table 2.1 The same voters' profile

Preferences	Number of voters and their preferences			
	5	4	3	2
1st	A	B	C	D
2nd	D	D	D	C
3rd	C	C	B	B
4th	B	A	A	A

So now let's look at some of the non-binary methodologies, and maybe the best way is to see what happens when we use them on the example we had in Table 1.1, now reproduced as Table 2.1. And, you will remember, we said options *A* and *B* were rather divisive, while *C* or *D* were more likely to best represent the voters' collective will. So let's analyse this voters' profile using different decision-making systems. Stand by for some mathematics... but not any difficult stuff.

2.2.1 Plurality Voting

The simplest form of multi-option voting is called plurality voting,[3] where there is a plurality of options, and in Table 2.1 there are four of them. The voter may choose just one option, and this he does by giving (not a ✓ but, for some strange reason) an × to the option she wants. The winner is the option with the most × 's. So in Table 2.1, the winner—the social choice, to use the technical term—is option *A*; and the social ranking—the options in order of supposed popularity, first to fourth—is *A–B–C–D*.

Now this winner, option *A*, cannot be called the democratic majority opinion, not in this example anyway, because its score of 5 is well short of a majority, 50% + 1, which would of course be 8 or more; 5 is only the largest minority. As a means of identifying a democratic majority opinion, therefore, plurality voting is often just not good enough. Another disadvantage of plurality voting lies in the fact that, in many political contests, the options may not be treated fairly, not least by the media—the latter often tends to concentrate on what they regard as the favourites. This in turn may mean that some voters will be tempted to vote 'tactically'—again I use the technical term—lest their opinion be regarded as 'a wasted vote'.

---

[3] The equivalent electoral system is first-past-the-post, FPTP.

2.2.2 The Two-Round System

In order to ensure that the winning option does actually have majority support, resort is sometimes made to a two-round system, TRS.[4] If nothing has a majority in the first-round plurality vote—as is the case in Table 2.1— we take the two leading options from that plurality vote—option **A** on 5 and **B** on 4—and hold a second-round majority vote between these two. In our own example, then, the final is between **A** and **B**, and if everyone votes again with the same preferences, the winner of the second round is option **B** on a score of 9. And 9, of course, *is* a majority.

2.2.3 The Alternative Vote

Another way of doing things is called the alternative vote AV, or preference voting PV in Australasia, or instant run-off voting IRV or ranked choice voting RCV in North America.[5] This is another knock-out system, though possibly of many rounds.

The voters now cast their preferences—1, 2, 3..., as many as they wish— and the count consists of a number of plurality votes. If no-one option has a majority of 1st preferences, the least popular option is eliminated and its votes are transferred to its voters' 2nd preference option(s)... and this process continues until one option does have a majority. In the first plurality vote, which we call stage (i), the social ranking is **A–B–C–D**, 5–4–3–2— so nothing has a majority; we therefore eliminate the smallest option, **D**, and transfer its 2 votes to its voters' 2nd preference, option **C**. This gives us a stage (ii) score line of **A–B–C**, 5–4–5. Still nothing with a majority, so option **B** is now out, and its 4 votes go to... well they can't go to their 2nd preference of **D** because **D** has been eliminated, so they go to the 4 **B**'s voters' 3rd preference, option **C**. The stage (iii) score line is thus **A–C**, 5–9, so the winner is **C** on a score of 9 which, as we know, is indeed a majority. The AV democratic majority opinion, option **C**, is not the same as the TRS democratic majority opinion, option **B**, so maybe one of these voting procedures is inadequate. Maybe both of them are.

---

[4] This too can be used as an electoral system, as in France.

[5] It is also called the single transferable vote, STV, although this latter acronym normally applies when it is being used as an electoral system, especially in its PR (proportional representation) format—PR-STV.

2.2.4   Serial Voting

Yet another knock-out system is called serial voting. If we are debating, let's say, tax rates, if the status quo is 50% and if someone suggests 60, while another wants 45 and yet another prefers 40%, then these four options could all be arranged in order: 60–50–45–40; and just to make it all balanced, we could add a fifth option of 55% so that it reads: 60–55–50–45–40. (Needless to say, we couldn't do this with the vegetables from Chap. 1; with tax rates, however, it is certainly possible.)

Serial voting is a series of majority votes between the two options at either end, between 60 and 40 in this instance. The loser is eliminated, and the second vote is between the two subsequent extremes—either 55 and 40 or 60 and 45—and the process continues until just one option remains. The outcome of a serial vote is always the Condorcet winner (para 2.2.8)… if there is one.

In our own example, if the options were placed in order *A–B–C–D*, then *D* wins the first round, *A* v *D*, by 9:5. Next is *B* v *D*, which *D* also wins, 10:4. Hence the final is *C* v *D*, and *D* is again on top, 11:3. So the overall winner is *D*.

2.2.5   Approval Voting

Approval voting is a non-preferential multi-option voting procedure. The punter may 'approve' of an option if he thinks it is brilliant, or adequate, or even just tolerable. So some voters may approve of just one option, and others may approve of a few. This means of course that those who vote for only their favourite option have a greater chance of seeing their favourite succeed. In contrast, those who support two or a few options may actually reduce their 1st preference favourite's chances of winning. Approval voting can work well when everybody is already in a consensual frame of mind; it is not so appropriate, however, for the rough and tumble of politics.

A further disadvantage lies in the fact that the count of an approval vote may be conducted in a number of different ways. We can take either all the 1st and 2nd preferences as approvals, in which case, in our example, the winner is option *D* on a score of 14, while the social ranking is *D–A/C–B* with scores of *D*-14, *A/C*-5, *B*-4; or we can count all the 1st, 2nd and 3rd preferences, in which case the social choice is a *C/D* draw, both on 14, and the social ranking is *C/D–B–A*—and their scores are now *C/D*-14, *B*-9, *A*-5. Two very different results!

In many instances, an approval vote social choice will nevertheless be a democratic majority opinion, but there may be more than one; indeed, it might take the mathematician a little time to sort it all out.

2.2.6   Range Voting

A 'difficult to define' methodology—preferential or non-preferential or whatever—is range voting. Here the voter is given, say, 10 points, which she can distribute at will. The extremist will be tempted to plonk all 10 points onto his favourite, while the more consensual voter might give 5 points to her favourite, 3 to a good compromise and 2 to her 3rd choice, or whatever.

As in approval voting, therefore, the methodology discourages those who would wish for consensus and encourages the intransigent to remain so. In a word, it is totally unsuited to the political forum. What's more, it's also almost impossible to analyse.

2.2.7   The Borda Count and Modified Borda Count

There are a few preferential systems in which, as in AV, the voters may cast their preferences, 1, 2, 3… as they wish, maybe up to a maximum of, say, six options. The first of these voting systems is a points system, the Borda count BC or modified Borda count MBC, (the difference between these two systems is described in para 2.4 and demonstrated in para 4.6). The preferences are translated into points—in a 4-option ballot, a 1st preference can get 4 points, a 2nd 3, etc.—the points are added, and the winner is the option with the most.

In our own example, option **A** with five 1st preferences and nine 4th preferences gets a score of

$$(5 \times 4) + (9 \times 1) = 20 + 9 = 29 \text{ points;}$$

while **D** gets two 1st and a dozen 2nd preferences, which is

$$(2 \times 4) + (12 \times 3) = 8 + 36 = 44 \text{ points.}$$

So the winner is option **D**, and the social ranking is **D–C–B–A** with scores **D**-44, **C**-36, **B**-31, **A**-29. Umm, sounds good; but there is a little problem, (para 2.4).

As we shall see, for a winning option to be accepted, the MBC relies on it gaining a reasonable margin of popularity over the other options. If in the above example, the scores were 36, 35, 35 and 34, the Speaker would obviously conclude that there was no consensus, and there's more on all this in para 3.2.7, when we talk of average preference scores and consensus coefficients. Indeed, once we go into the mathematics of it all—which is where it belongs, in Annex IV.2—we will see that the MBC is indeed a precision instrument, able to identify (if such an outcome does actually exist) the best compromise or, at a higher threshold, the consensus, or at the highest level, the collective wisdom.

Suffice to say at this stage that, in consensus politics, a mean score is just not good enough; we'll have none of that 50% +1 unAfrican nonsense. Rather, good Lord, we can have consensus, today! And if we can't find it in debate, let us at least try to identify it in a preferential ballot.

2.2.8   The Condorcet Rule

Finally, there is the Condorcet rule. Again, the voter casts his preferences, and the count examines all the pairings (para 1.1)—*A/B, A/C… C/D*—all six of them, to see which option wins the most pairings. By looking at Table 2.1, we can see that *B > A, C > A* and *D > A*, and also that *C > B, D > B* and *D > C*. So, in total, *D* wins 3 pairings, *C* wins 2, *B* has 1 and *A* gets none.

In this example, and whenever there is no paradox, when one option wins all the pairings, all of which are in effect majority votes, then the Condorcet winner is definitely the democratic majority opinion. In other instances, we take the winner as the option which wins the most pairings, and this is called the Copeland winner… which might identify the most popular option.

2.3   An Overall Comparison

In summary, with multi-option voting, the outcome could be, again, *A* or *B* or *C* or *D*. So we should use a methodology which this comparison tells us is a good one, lest the choice of voting system be yet another instance of manipulation. The results are summarised in Table 2.2.

The BC/MBC and Condorcet are the only two systems which *always* take *all* preferences cast by *all* voters into account. Little wonder, then, that they are the most accurate. The MBC can identify the option with the highest average preference, while Condorcet identifies the option which wins the most pairings.

Table 2.2 Various voting procedures' outcomes

Voting Procedures		Social Choice	Social Ranking			
Plurality voting		A	A-5	B-4	C-3	D-2
TRS		B	B-9	A-5		
AV/IRV/PV/RCV/STV		C	C-9	A-5		
Serial Voting (*A-B-C-D*)		D	D-11	C-3		
Approval Voting	1st/2nd	D	D-14	A/C-5		B-4
	1st/2nd/3rd	C/D	C/D-14		B-9	A-5
Range voting		?	?			
BC/MBC		D	D-44	C-36	B-31	A-29
Condorcet		D	D-3	C-2	B-1	A-0

2.3.1 Choice

It is also worth noting that, in a binary vote, the choice is **A** or **B**, so there are just two ways of voting, (either that or abstain). When there are three options—**A, B,** and **C**—as in a plurality vote, the voter may have a choice of three ways of voting, but in any preferential vote, there are six ways of completing a three-option ballot: **A–B–C, A–C–B, B–A–C, B–C–A, C–A–B** and **C–B–A**. With four options—**A, B, C** and **D**—there are 24 different ways in which the voter may submit a full ballot, and with five options, up to 120 different opinions and nuances may be expressed. It's called pluralism.

Admittedly, with the tax rates of (para 2.2.4), there may not be quite that many rational opinions. To vote 45–55–40–60–50, for example, (Graph III.1), would be rather illogical, and could prompt some to think the voter was drunk or drugged. There are nevertheless 14 different logical sets of preferences, which we call single-peaked curves (and they're in Table 3.2).

2.4 Consensus Voting

Now some politicians, as we've already said quite often, are manipulative… but so too are some voters. When faced with a multi-option ballot, they may be tempted to vote 'tactically' rather than 'sincerely' (to use the technical jargon again). Such may certainly happen in a plurality vote, as was noted in para 2.2.1, with any favourites.

And such may also happen in an MBC: if a voter thinks that his 2nd preference might beat his 1st preference, he may cast his actual 2nd preference for something else, and give his real 2nd preference his last preference. For this reason, the rules for the conduct of an MBC cater for composites (which we shall discuss in Chap. 3) and partial voting, which we'll deal with here.

Now in an MBC of four options, as noted, a 1st preference gets 4 points, a 2nd gets 3, and so on… if, that is the voter has cast all four preferences. If, however, he has listed only one option, then his favourite gets just 1 point; if she has listed two preferences, then her favourite gets 2 points and her 2nd choice gets 1 point. And so on.

Basically, in a ballot of four options,

- he who casts only one preference gets his favourite 1 point;
- she who casts two preferences gets her favourite 2 points (and her 2nd choice 1 point);
- and so on; accordingly;
- those who cast all four preferences get their favourite 4 points, (their 2nd choice 3 points, etc.).

To put it all into mathematical language—as promised in the Preface, this text includes just one formula, and here it is: in a ballot of n options, a voter may cast m preferences, and obviously,

$$n \geq m \geq 1$$

Points shall be awarded to (1st, 2nd … last) preferences cast, according to the rule

$$(m, m - 1 \ldots 1). \tag{\{rule(i)\}}$$

Unfortunately, this was changed to

$$(n, n - 1 \ldots 1), \tag{\{rule(ii)\}}$$

or even,

$$(n - 1, n - 2 \ldots 0). \tag{\{rule(iii)\}}$$

so the voter could cast just his 1st preference, get the full 4 points, and ignore the rest. The m rule, ({rule(i)}), encourages everyone to participate in the democratic process and to the full, to recognise the validity of the other options, and to imply that they will accept the outcome, even if the latter

is not their favourite. The n rules, in contrast, ({rule(ii)})} and ({rule(iii)}},
may[6] encourage intransigence, just like approval voting.

2.4.1 The Right Answer

The m rule is the Modified Borda Count, and it is what the inventor, Jean-
Charles de Borda, actually advocated. Now admittedly, if everyone fills in
a full list of preferences, then there's no difference between the two voting
procedures—BC or MBC: both the social choice and the social ranking are
the same in both procedures. If some voters, and especially if lots of voters,
submit only partial ballots, however, the BC voting procedure may no longer
facilitate the identification of the collective will. Indeed, at worst, if everyone
casts just a 1st preference—and this is the incentive with those n rules—the
BC is almost the same as a plurality vote.

The MBC, in contrast, encourages every voter to cast a full list of preferences; and if an option's MBC score passes a certain threshold—more of all
this in Annex IV—then that option will definitely represent the democratic
majority opinion.

In effect, the MBC prompts the voter to submit a full ballot, and because
of the possibility of compositing (para 3.2.5), the MBC encourages the voter
to vote sincerely and not tactically. Admittedly, the voter who wants to
manipulate can still try: so he who wants Northern Ireland to be devolved
within the UK, and whose 2nd preference is a unitary state UK, could
nevertheless give his 2nd preference to a unitary state united Ireland… yer
wha'? He's not going to do that! And nor is the Unionist politician going to
campaign for his supporters to give a 2nd preference for such an option.

Simple decision-making systems are easy to manipulate; sophisticated ones
are much more difficult and, as this book proceeds, increasingly so.

2.5 Not Yet Nirvana

Now nothing's perfect, of course. But some systems are less imperfect than
others. And if, as we said in para 1.2, option D best represents the collective social choice, and if we also conclude that the true social ranking is
D–C–B–A, then plurality voting, which produces the exact opposite, a social
ranking of A–B–C–D, is wrong, hopelessly wrong… indeed, it couldn't be

---

[6] Whether or not rule ({rule(ii)}) or rule ({rule(iii)}) is used, there is, of course, no difference in the
resulting social ranking; in the scores, yes, but not in the actual ranking.

Table 2.3 The threesome again, on four options

Preferences	Ms *i*	Mr *j*	Ms *k*
1st	A	B	C
2nd	B	C	D
3rd	C	D	A
4th	D	A	B

Table 2.4 The same threesome, on three options

Preferences	Ms *i*	Mr *j*	Ms *k*
1st	A	B	C
2nd	B	C	A
3rd	C	A	B

more wrong; it's 'more-wrong-ish' or moronic. (The same logic applies to the FPTP electoral system. It too is plain stupid, as we shall see in Chap. 5.)

So plurality voting is not the best. It follows that any systems which are based on plurality voting—TRS and AV/IRV/PV/RCV/STV—are also imperfect. OK, some of them can nearly always produce a democratic majority opinion but, as we saw in Table 2.2, it might not be the correct democratic majority opinion. We also know that approval voting, which can identify more than one democratic majority opinion, actually discourages the consensual while range voting is worse in that it incentivises the extremist.

So let's stick with the MBC and Condorcet: they are accurate, but they too have their weaknesses. The MBC is prone to what is called an irrelevant alternative, which we'll look at more closely in Annex IV. Briefly, it's like this. If we look again at Table 1.2 in para 1.3.1, which now becomes Table 2.3, we see that everybody prefers **C** to **D**. So we could say that **D** is therefore irrelevant and we can remove it. In which case, the voters' profile would look like Table 2.4.

With Table 2.3 where a 1st preference gets 4 points, a 2nd gets 3, etc., the MBC scores are as follows:

$$A = 4 + 2 + 1 = 7$$
$$B = 4 + 3 + 1 = 8$$
$$C = 4 + 3 + 2 = 9$$
$$D = 3 + 2 + 1 = 6$$

but with Table 2.4, where a 1st preference gets 3 points, a 2nd gets 2, etc., the MBC scores are as follows:

$$A = 3 + 2 + 1 = 6$$
$$B = 3 + 2 + 1 = 6$$
$$C = 3 + 2 + 1 = 6$$

So, if you (add or) subtract an irrelevant alternative, you might change the result; with option **D** rendered irrelevant, what was a social choice of **C** and a social ranking of **C–B–A–D**, becomes a dead heat social choice and ranking of **A/B/C**. Likewise, if a clone is added to the list of options on the ballot paper, option **E**, a clone of one of the other options or whatever, then again, the social choice and ranking might be different.

2.6 Conclusion

The MBC is prone to the irrelevant alternative, unlike the Condorcet rule. But Condorcet may suffer from the paradox, to which the MBC is immune. So, the best possible voting procedure—and I'm by no means the first to suggest this[7]—the most robust and accurate methodology for use in every Congress or Parliament on the planet, the decision-making forum in a one-, two- or multi-party state, could be a combined MBC/Condorcet analysis. Then, if the social choices from both analyses are identical, all concerned may rest assured: this indeed is the collective will. Perfect. Well, 99% perfect.

The collective will of Congress/Parliament? That sounds like a different sort of politics. Let's start a new chapter and see how it would work in practice.

---

[7] Others include Charles Dodgson and Duncan Black, of whom there's more in Chap. 6.

3

The Art and Science of Compromise

The truth of an Assembly's decisions depends as much on the form by which they are reached as on the enlightenment of its members.

Le Marquis de Condorcet
quoted by I. McLean, Arnold B. Urken in
Classics of Social Choice (1995, p. 113).

Abstract Identifying the will of any decision-making chamber requires a good number of rules and regulations. These should ensure that every party may participate in the formation of a list of options, that each contributor is given an equal opportunity to state their opinion, that all the options are given a fair hearing, that the final ballot paper fairly represents every valid proposal, that all concerned may express their views accurately and that the subsequent analysis is also accurate. All of that said, the rules for a consensus debate may actually be fewer than those required for a debate which concludes with an illogical and inaccurate binary ballot.

Keywords Collective will · Inclusive politics · Consensus coefficients · Win-win decision-making

3.1 Introduction

The nature of any debate is often determined by the nature of the decision-making process with which that debate concludes. If that final decision is to be a divisive, 'for' or 'against' binary vote, the debate itself may well be adversarial (para 1.4); in contrast, a preferential vote may be the catalyst of a more nuanced and rational exchange.

The goal, of course, is to identify the participants' democratic majority opinion. This has often been defined in a number of different ways: some call it the will of the majority, while a more precise definition could be as follows: it is that option which

- seeks to bring the greatest good to the greatest number;
- is most agreeable to all;
- is the most acceptable compromise; or
- best represents the consensus.

Or again, given the arguments debated in Chap. 2, we could describe it as the option which gains the voters' highest average preference. This we now know is what the modified Borda count MBC can achieve, so let's look at how it all works in practice. Consider a multi-party parliament (or a multi-faction, or multi-faceted, or multi-ethnic one-party congress) with let's say six parties (factions/groups/ethnicities) represented.

3.2   The Consensus Debate

We start on the understanding that a Speaker and Deputy have already been elected (in accordance with a consensual electoral system, as described in Chap. 5); that the rules which we outline below are all laid down in a set of Standing Orders; that all members present are registered and eligible to participate in the debate, each with an equal allocation of time[1] and, if the debate ends in a vote, each able to cast their preferences in a free vote, for the purpose of which each has a very smart phone. In addition, the rules shall state that no-one member or party or minority has the right of veto; rather, that everyone, including the majority, has a responsibility to seek that which is best for the common good.[2]

---

[1] Everyone is subject to a time limitation. This may be best effected with a set of lights because, after all, you can't shout out a light. So each participant shall be allocated a fixed number of minutes—x minutes for a proposer, y for everyone else. When each starts, the light is green; at say one minute remaining, it turns to amber; and then it goes red... but if the speaker still rambles on, it gets brighter and brighter, the longer he transgresses his rights.

Likewise, in any consensus debate on the web, contributions shall be limited in both number and word length. There are no filibusters in a consensus debate.

[2] One possible but rather impractical methodology to ensure all concerned maintain a certain decorum is to ask every member of parliament to have a cat on his lap, gently purring in feline contentment, while the members participate in a peaceful, pleasant dia- or better still, 'poly-logue'. If any member

Maybe the biggest difference between a binary and a consensual debate in this: in the former, with that final vote destined to be a majority vote, participants will not want to declare their 2nd preferences, so chances of coming to a compromise are few. If however the decision is to be based on an MBC, then participants may state their 2nd and 3rd preferences, without such statements detracting from what is still their 1st preference. Then, with all cards laid on the table, it will be obvious to all where lies the compromise… if, that is, there is one.

It also follows that, in any pre-election campaign, in consensus politics, parties should not make policy promises in the form of single options. If the aim is to be in a multi-party parliament and cabinet, in an all-party power-sharing executive (which we come to in the next chapter), then policies will be decided in consensus. Each party may have its ideals, of course, but it should also be prepared to compromise… accordingly, it should state its views as a set of preferences. Having read Chap. 5, it might want to declare that its 1st preference electoral system is the Irish system of proportional representation PR, but its second preference is the Swiss model, and its third the Dutch version (para E.2).

3.2.1 The Structure of the Debate

No matter what the forum, a parliament or congress, a public enquiry or a citizens' assembly, be it virtual and on the web, or be it in person, the guidelines for conducting a consensual debate are pretty much the same.

Initially, when a problem arises in, say, a parliament of some 200 members, there may be up to 200 different points of view as to a possible solution. When a public enquiry is set up, there may be thousands of opinions. The purpose of the debate or enquiry is to identify, just the one single option or prioritisation that might best represent all of these opinions, or, as happened in New Zealand's independent commission on their electoral system in 1992,[3] a representative short list of about five options, which was then put to the people in a multi-option referendum.

---

starts to behave noisily, to wave his arms, to gesticulate, to swear even… then oops, up jumps the cat… and he is no longer allowed to speak. Yes, it's a little impractical.

[3] The Commission settled for five options, ranging from FPTP (the British system of first-past-the-post, which was the old status quo) to the Irish form of a preferential PR, with three options as it were in the middle, (para 2.2, Footnote 3). Sure enough, in an unusual form of a two-round referendum, the result was a compromise—a 50:50 mixture of FPTP and PR, the German system: it got 58% of a 55% turnout in the first round, and 54 of 83% in the second. See also para 5.2.2, Footnote 3.

For the moment, let's stick to the parliamentary scenario. We can start to reduce this wide variety of ideas by limiting the number of options to one per party/faction/fraction. Let's assume someone(s) move a possible solution, a motion, which we'll call option **A**. Other parties might want to change things a little, or quite a bit, or maybe a lot. Whatever their ideas, they don't just seek amendments to this or that clause of that or this sub-section of this or that paragraph, each to be resolved in a binary vote; rather, they submit a complete package.[4] Accordingly, in a parliament of let's say eight parties, there might well be eight options 'on the table'—let's say options **A** to **H**— all summarised on a computer screen and, if required, written out in full and explained on a dedicated website. In practice, of course, it is likely that two of the smaller parties might combine to propose a joint option, but we'll start with a full list of eight.

If the difference between option **A** and the first alternative, option **B**, is quite small, the complete package can be almost the same as option **A**, with any variations in the option-**B**-package merely highlighted in a different tint. Where the difference is more substantial—in option **C**, say—it would still be advisable for this option **C** to be submitted in a similar format.

Suffice to say that every option is allowed, one per party, as long as it is relevant to the debate and complies with a previously agreed norm like the United Nations UN Charter on Human Rights. We are talking about inclusive politics, so 'every (relevant) thing is on the table', (as is sometimes said in peace negotiations).

3.2.2 Choosing the Options

In the debate itself, participants may propose to tweak or amend or change any part of any proposed option; moreover, if two options are fairly similar, anyone can suggest a composite of the two; later on, it might get to a stage when everyone agrees that one of the options may now be deleted. Everything is possible. But the important thing is this: nothing changes unless the original proposer(s) agree(s) to such a change!

As the debate proceeds, therefore, so the options on the table will vary, both in substance and in number. What had been **A, B, C, D, E, F, G** and **H** might become **A′, B, C′, D, F, G** and **H** and later still **A′, C″, F, G** and **H**.

---

[4] Something similar happens in the German *Bundestag* (parliament) when the members are choosing a new Chancellor. If any party wishes to criticise the first proposal for Chancellor **A**, they must be positive and propose an alternative, Chancellor **B**. They don't just vote 'no' (as they did in the Weimar Republic, which *inter alia* enabled Hitler to come to power).

In some debates, it might even happen that the number of options comes down to a singleton... in which case, this may be seen as the will of parliament, the verbal consensus and... next business.

Usually, however, disagreements will abound. So, when every option still on the table has had a good hearing, the Speaker might suggest a ballot. He shall first draw up a (short) list of about five options, a balanced list as best represents the debate. If all concerned are content with this list, if every original proposer is happy that her option has been included either verbatim or in composite, (or at the very least has been considered before being deleted with her consent), all may proceed to the vote, a multi-option preferential vote.

As we said in para 2.4, the MBC encourages the voter to cast all his preferences. The impartial Speaker has already decided that the options listed are all legitimate aspirations, compliant with the UN Charter. In casting their five preferences, therefore, each member of the parliament may also, in effect, recognise the validity of these various aspirations; in addition, she as it were implies that if the consensus of the House is not her own 1st preference but one of the other options, that she will nevertheless not only accept this result, but also help to ensure that this democratic collective will is implemented.

If the average preference score of the winning option is greater than a predetermined threshold—of which, there's more in para IV.2—this result may then be enacted. By the executive. Which is why it has this name. In a democracy, by definition, the people are at the top; next comes their congress or parliament; and at the bottom of this hierarchy comes the executive whose job, on all non-urgent matters, is to implement the will of the House or, if the vote has been put to a referendum, the will of the people.

3.2.3 Maintaining a Balance

When the Speaker is drawing up a ballot, she should follow certain guidelines. If the members are debating the lunch menu, the list of possible vegetables can be as long as a runner bean—every suggestion of every party or even participant may be included. On a more complex topic, however, the budget or certain aspects of Climate Change, say, maybe there are lots of options on the table, in which case the (short) list should be balanced and limited in number, probably to at least four and at most six options.

First of all, therefore, we'll consider a guideline on how to draw up a balanced list. Let's take another simple example: if the parliament is debating tax rates for the rich, as we did in para 2.2.4, the debate could in theory range from 0% (as desired by some of the very rich) to 100% (as a few of their opponents might wish), but it will probably focus on a range of options somewhere in the middle, let's say, between 40 and 60%. Now in a rather lop-sided parliament, a list of eight options on the table might be 40, 50, 53, 55, 57, 58, 59 and 60—anything is possible—but a fair list might reduce this to a list of just a few options, let's say three, four, five or six options:

$$40-50-60$$
$$40-46.7-53.3-60$$
$$40-45-50-55-60$$
or
$$40-44-48-52-56-60$$

To have only three options could perhaps be biased in favour of the one in the middle.[5] To have the four options as listed above, what with those decimal places, would be a bit cumbersome, especially if the participants have already agreed to seek a consensus to the nearest whole number (or at least 0.5%). So maybe the best choice would be either the above list of five options, or that of the six.

3.2.4 Casting a Vote

And here we come to one of the many advantages of the MBC. If a member of parliament wants a policy of exactly 50%, then of course, he could cast his 1st preference for that option of 50. But as we now know, it's wise to submit a full ballot in an MBC, so if we take the above five-option ballot, maybe he should vote 50–45–55–60–40 or 50–55–45–40–60, casting any lower preferences either side of 50 in equal weighting. If on the other hand she wants a policy of 53%, exactly, and if the ballot is still of the above five-option variety, then she could vote 50–55–60–45–40 (para II.2).

In other words, the MBC allows the voter to express his point of view with a fair degree of accuracy. (For an exact summary of how such a five-option ballot could be interpreted, in any one of 14 different logical ways, see Table III.1). This also means that it doesn't matter too much, whether the Speaker decides on a five- or a six-option ballot.[6]

---

[5] But not always. In 1931, Finland had a three-option referendum on alcohol: 'prohibition', 'a little relaxation' and 'abolition' of then existing restrictions. The compromise option got a miserable 1%, while abolition was supported by the cheers of 71%.

[6] Whereas, of course, as we saw in Chap. 1, in a binary ballot, everything depends on the question. If the ballot were on the above six-option ballot paper, he who wanted 50% exactly could vote 48–52–56–44–40–60 or 52–48–44–56–60–40.

In many ballots, the MBC seeks to persuade the voter to cast a full slate of preferences. If n the number of options is ≤ 10, then it is practical to do so and thus the voters are encouraged to recognise the validity of all of their neighbours' listed aspirations. If, however, $n > 10$, we recommend the rules lay down a maximum of 6 preferences.

When making a decision, the MBC social choice is the answer, if that is it surpasses the predetermined threshold. When making a prioritisation, a certain flexibility can be good: if the aim is to seek, let us say, the top six items, but if the results indicate a cluster of seven popular items, then maybe the chair might decide to include all seven. It all depends upon the rules laid down for each particular debate.

3.2.5 Analysing the Outcome

So, every member votes (ideally electronically). The voters' profile is displayed, and the Speaker then interprets these results, to determine the outcome. If the results indicate a dead heat between, say, options 50 and 55, then obviously, the precise social choice should be 52.5%. Or if the collective social ranking is 50–55–60–45–40, then the Speaker may conclude that the outcome is 53%, (as in Table III.1). Politics, they say, is the art of compromise; the MBC is its science.

Compromise, indeed, is an intrinsic part of the entire process. It might happen in debate, as options are changed or even composited. It may certainly happen in the vote, if members cast their lower preferences for what are, in effect, their compromise options. And it might also happen in the analysis, if and when the Speaker (in interpreting the collective social ranking) forms a composite. With tax rates, this is possible; with vegetables for lunch, possibly not; but on a whole range of other policies, on budgets and electoral systems (as we shall see in Chap. 5) and constitutional arrangements, compromise is often a possibility, if not a necessity.

3.2.6 Consensus Coefficients

Now let's return to the theory, and we again consider a five-option ballot. If every member of a committee of 12 persons casts a full list of preferences on a ballot of five options, then an option, let's say option A, which gets all twelve 1st preferences, will get an average preference score of 1.00. Another option, B, might get a dozen 5th preferences, to get an average preference score of 5.00. While option C might get a dozen 3rd preferences, and get the mean average preference score of 3.00.

In majority voting, some people argue that 50% + 1 is all that is required. In consensus politics, in contrast, we think such a mean score is too mean, (and statements to suggest that such an outcome is actually 'the will of the people' are often pretty meaningless). So, prior to the debate, the Speaker shall announce just what level of consensus or average preference score is required for the result to be regarded as binding. To do so, she could indeed use the above average preference scores; if, however, some voters have submitted only partial votes, measuring the averages doesn't work: too many zeros. She should therefore use a different measure, called the option's consensus coefficient CC, the ratio of its MBC score to the maximum possible score: for each option, it ranges from 1.00 which is excellent to 0.00 which implies there is no consensus at all; but all the mathematics, as promised, are in Annex IV.

With partial ballots, the absolute minimum average preference score of zero is achieved—(if that's the right word)—only if everybody gives the said option nothing at all, i.e. if it gets not a single preference from anyone. But this option would not be on the ballot paper if someone(s) had not proposed it; so presumably, these supporters will give it some preferences. The chances therefore of any option ever getting an average preference score of 0.00 should be zero.

In like manner, the chances of any option getting every voter's 1st preference—the maximum average preference score and a CC of 1.00—are also just about nil. Nevertheless, by measuring the CC, we can see which options are most popular. Furthermore, because it is highly unlikely that all five options can all be mutually exclusive of all the other five, the Speaker may well be able—and feel obliged—to composite any aspects of a second most popular option which are mutually compatible with the most popular one. With tax rates, this is all very straight forward; admittedly, when resolving other contentious subjects, this might not be so easy; nevertheless, even on vegetables for lunch, the chef might accept the possibility of a stir-fry compromise.

3.2.7   The Inclusive Average

We should also point out that, because the MBC identifies the option with the highest average preference, that it is therefore in everyone's vested interest to participate in the (debate and the) vote, in order to influence that average; there's more on all this in Annex IV as well. Indeed, the more you look at it, the more brilliant the MBC becomes…

Whether you identify the highest average preference, calculate the best CC, or find the summit of the collective single-peaked curve (Annex III), the MBC can give an accurate representation of the collective will—not least because it encourages everyone to vote sincerely and, in so doing, makes manipulation impractical if not next to impossible. Indeed, in some instances, it will be possible to calculate the collective CC so accurately that the Speaker will be able to categorise the outcome as 'the best compromise', 'the consensus' or 'the collective wisdom'. Umm, that definitely requires some maths… or maybe just a computer.

On the other hand, when things don't go so smoothly, it might happen that the options' CCs will make the Speaker decide that there is no consensus at all—the sort of 36–35–35–34 outcome which we saw in para 2.2.7—in which case, the debate may have to be adjourned and re-scheduled. The vote itself may nevertheless be regarded as a straw poll, with indications perhaps as to which options deserve further consideration. Furthermore, when discussing a really complicated topic, it might be quite useful to have a straw poll every so often, just to see what is the collective mood, so that all are aware of any progress made.

3.3   The Speaker

As you might have gathered, the Speaker in this sort of consensus debate is often pretty busy. She first has to decide whether or not the proposed options are relevant and, if so, do they comply with the UN Charter. She may also have to advise any party wishing to propose an alternative option as to the desired format. Then she has to compile a list of these options, bearing in mind the fact that the list must (soon, or at least eventually) be balanced.

If the participants agree to change any of the options in any way, she may well have to alter that list, while still maintaining this balance. Later, if she decides the list should be put to a vote, she has to prepare the ballot which, as we mentioned, if the subject is complex, may well be just a short list of no more than six options; and only when all are agreed that this list fairly represents the debate should she ask everyone to move to a vote and cast their preferences. If need be, prior to the vote, she should announce how various sets of preferences may be interpreted, (para III.2), and declare the average preference threshold required for an outcome to be binding. She might even state the levels at which an outcome may be classified on a scale ranging from 'no consensus' via 'best possible compromise' and 'consensus' to 'collective wisdom' (paras 4.7 and 5.6).

When the voting has been completed—which, if it is done electronically, need take no longer than a nanosecond or few—she must display the voters' profile and analyse the results; if the threshold has been surpassed, she may conclude with a definite outcome and its precise CC. The executive may then execute.

Given all of this, the Speaker may need not only a Deputy, but also a few assistants.

Some might argue that this makes life very complicated, which to a certain extent is true. Suffice here to say that binary voting is often far more complicated. By asking just a binary question, the Brexit vote in the UK led to four years (and more) of bitter debate which culminated in a very unsatisfactory, inaccurate (and perhaps temporary) conclusion. As we mentioned earlier, other binary votes led to even more protracted and horrible consequences: violence and wars.

3.4   Conclusion

When the debate and vote have been completed, and a single policy option has been agreed to, the entire process is at an end: 200 or more opinions were distilled, firstly into eight fairly quickly; next, more slowly perhaps, these were whittled down to a list of six, then five options, and eventually to just one—the social choice. It might not be the 1st preference of very many, but if from a final list of five options it is the 2nd preference of lots and maybe the 3rd preference of a few as well, it might indeed be the option or a composite which best represents the collective consensus. Furthermore, with its average preference score, all concerned may know, precisely, its level of collective support.

Reference

McLean, I., & Urken, A. B. (1995). *Classics of social choice*. Ann Arbor: The University of Michigan Press, Michigan.

4

The Goat is a Gnu*—Electing an All-Party Power-Sharing Executive

... it must be demanded that there be some sort of consensus...
Kenneth J. Arrow
Social Choice and Individual Values (1963, p. 83).

Abstract The preferential points decision-making voting system is more accurate than binary and most other forms of voting used in decision-making; therefore, it is more democratic; therefore again, it should be the basis of governance. Now this methodology can identify the option with the highest *average* preference... and an average, of course, includes *every* member of the chamber, not just a majority of them. Accordingly, the government should represent not a divided but the *entire* parliament, and an all-party power-sharing government of national unity may in fact be the most democratic form of majority rule. But how best can a parliament choose such an inclusive executive? The democratic way is via an election—a preferential, proportional, two-dimensional, matrix vote.

Keywords Governance · Majority rule · Conflict resolution · Power-sharing · Matrix vote · Consensual polity

---

*Government of All the Talents, and Government of National Unity.

© The Author(s), under exclusive license to Springer Nature Switzerland AG 2022
P. Emerson, *The Punters' Guide to Democracy*,
https://doi.org/10.1007/978-3-031-06987-1_4

4.1   Introduction

It is extraordinary fact of life but, in the name of majority rule, many countries are sometimes ruled by just one individual—minorities of one. In fact, in a two-party state in which both parties select their leader in a majoritarian procedure, it may well be that he who leads the bigger 'half' of the bigger party then becomes the president or prime minister. But a half of a half is only a quarter; 51% of 51% is only 26%; so sometimes, 'majority rule' as practiced is actually a form of a minority diktat.

If that individual is then able to (go into the closet and) choose his (praetorian guard or) cabinet,[1] and if that executive then decides which binary questions shall be put to the parliament, having first told his whip[2] that his MPs must vote (not perhaps as they or their constituents would wish, but) as he demands, the whole system becomes an 'elected dictatorship', to coin an oft-used phrase.

In a real majority rule democracy, excessive power would never be concentrated in the hands of just one person; it should first be separated into the well-known threesome: the judiciary, the legislature and the executive; secondly, at least in the two latter categories, power should be shared, and this can best be effected in a multi-party coalition.

Now many company boards and trades union executives and so on manage to do their business without first dividing into two opposing factions. Instead, the collective ensures that each office bearer is accountable to the whole. A parliament could easily do likewise. Governance could be based on a broad coalition—indeed, as in times of war and other emergencies, it often is—so all the members could regard themselves as members of a single team, chosen to pursue the best interests of all their citizens who have (by whatever means) chosen them.[3] To ensure the members do cooperate, parliament should use a voting procedure which encourages such cooperation: the House should

---

[1] In like manner, Vladimir Putin chooses his 'advisers', chronic cronies from his KGB days.

[2] I think the word 'whip' is an old nautical term. In the days of sail, a sailor deemed guilty of a crime was sometimes tied to the rigging, stripped to the waist, and whipped. In the most severe instances, the whip had three tails, each of which often drew blood. And hence today's use of the word: a whip may impose a 'three-line whip'—which (supposedly) all members must obey, lest they lose the whip. The word of three tails has three meanings.

[3] It is often said that governments must be held accountable, that an opposition is a vital part of any democracy; it is an argument which implies that everything is binary. It forgets that nearly every party is itself a coalition of different individuals, each of whom as it were holds their own colleagues to account. And it forgets the individual rivalries which have beset nearly every political party on the planet, not least—to take an extreme example—those which beset the dreaded Bolsheviks a century ago, between Lenin and Stalin; next, between Stalin and Trotsky; and later between Stalin and Bukharin—every clash a contest of two titans.

be a forum in which decisions on all non-urgent matters are based on those options which surpass a predetermined threshold of consensus coefficient or average preference score.

So how can a parliament choose a government, an all-party power-sharing coalition, one in which not only is every individual minister well suited to his/her portfolio, but every party in that parliament is represented in its proportional due? That's a daunting task.

4.2   The Matrix Vote

So let's take a simple example: imagine a club or an association of just eight persons, electing an executive committee of five office bearers. Let the individuals concerned be four males, Ed, Fred, Ned and Ted, along with four females, Breda, Eda, Freda and Veda. And let the five offices be the chair, vice-chair, secretary, treasurer and press officer.

4.2.1   The Matrix Vote—The Ballot

Now it goes without saying that not all eight of them are brilliant at everything. Fred, let's say, is literate but largely innumerate; he could perhaps be a good secretary but a lousy treasurer. Freda, in contrast, is numerate but next to illiterate—a good treasurer perhaps, but not such an able secretary. So what we need is a two-dimensional ballot paper, one on which every individual member at the annual general meeting AGM can choose, in order of preference, both those whom they want to be on the executive, and the office in which they wish each nominee to serve. The ballot paper should therefore be something like the one we have in Table 4.1.

Table 4.1   A matrix vote ballot

Preferences		Offices				
	Names	Chair	Vice	Secretary	Treasurer	Press
1st						
2nd						
3rd						
4th						
5th						

4.2.2   The Matrix Vote—The Vote

Different people might undertake this vote in different ways. One person might think the role of treasurer is the most important, so that office gets her 1st preference, as too, of course, the person she nominates for that office. Another member might think that Breda is the most capable of all the eight, so she gets his 1st preference, in whatever post he thinks suits her best. And so on. Everyone follows their own logic or even conscience and, as the old Yorkshire saying goes, 'there's nought as queer as folks'.

So each lists five different names in the shaded column and then gives five ticks, one to each nominee, whomsoever they think should be in whichsoever post. An example of a completed ballot is shown in Table 4.2; it consists of five different names in the shaded column, along with five ticks in the matrix, one in each column and one in each row.

4.2.3   The Matrix Vote—The Count

The count is conducted in two parts, and all according to the rules laid down for a modified Borda count MBC. Part (i) is an analysis of the preferences in that shaded column; part (ii) deciphers the data in the matrix.

Let's take the scenario of all eight persons submitting valid full ballots, each of five preferences. Every vote is therefore worth $5 + 4 + 3 + 2 + 1 = 15$ points, so the total number of points cast by all eight committee members is $8 \times 15 = 120$. And let's now assume, firstly, that part (i), the MBC analysis of the preferences shown in the left-hand shaded column, is complete… and lots of candidates have tied, but that's because I'm keeping the maths simple, with every sum a multiple of 5—and secondly, that the preferences cast in the matrix have been turned into points and added into sums. In all, let us also assume the initial tally of all the preferences-now-points cast is as shown in Table 4.3.

Veda is in first place, on a score of 20; so she is definitely elected to the committee… even though she's regarded as a bit of a dilettante, so we don't

Table 4.2   A completed matrix vote bllot

Preferences		Offices				
	Names	Chair	Vice	Secretary	Treasurer	Press
1st	Eda				✓	
2nd	Freda		✓			
3rd	Fred					✓
4th	Ned	✓				
5th	Ted			✓		

Table 4.3 The first matrix vote tally

| MBC | Names | Offices | | | | | MBC scores |
		Chair	Vice	Secretary	Treasurer	Press	
2nd =	Breda	5	5	5			15
7th =	Ed		5	5			10
2nd =	Eda	15					15
2nd =	Fred			15			15
2nd =	Freda		5		15		15
2nd =	Ned	5			5	5	15
7th =	Ted	5				5	10
1st	Veda	5	5		5	5	20
	MBC scores	35	20	25	25	15	120

yet know which office will be hers. And lots of committee members—Breda, Eda, Fred, Freda and Ned—all tie on joint second... so far. But the executive committee is to consist of only five office holders, so with Veda in, one of these second-placed members is going to lose out. Ah well, that's politics. While Ed and Ted, both in seventh place, are definitely out.

4.2.4 The Matrix Vote—The Analysis

Now we come to part (ii), the appointment of the successful candidates to the various offices, and this is done by an analysis of the sums shown in the matrix itself. We start with the biggest: 15, shown in Table 4.3 in green. And there are three of them, a tie! But there's no contention. Eda becomes the chair, Fred will do what he's good at, all the secretarial stuff, and Freda is given the purse strings, which is her natural talent.

These appointments mean that all the other data in Eda's, Fred's and Freda's columns and rows, become redundant. So the picture becomes clearer, as in Table 4.4.

That's three appointments done, and two to go, with three candidates still in the running; yes, one person has to lose. The next highest sum—indeed, the only remaining sum—is 5, and there are four of them, as shown. But

Table 4.4 The second matrix vote tally

| MBC | Names | Offices | | | | | MBC scores |
		Chair	Vice	Secretary	Treasurer	Press	
2nd =	Breda		5				15
2nd =	Eda	15					15
2nd =	Fred			15			15
2nd =	Freda				15		15
2nd =	Ned					5	15
1st	Veda		5			5	20
	MBC scores	35	20	25	25	15	120

there's still no problem: we take first the more popular candidate, which is Veda, and appoint her to… but she has 5 points for each of two potential posts, vice-chair and press, another tie. Yet again, there's no problem, for as we see in the bottom row, the office of vice-chair gets a bigger MBC score, 20, than that of Press, which gets only 15. So that's that: Veda becomes the vice-chair. That leaves Breda and Ned both competing for the final office, press, for which Ned has 5 points but Breda has none, so Ned gets the last post.

4.2.5   The Matrix Vote—The Result

The final result—and please note, I've now adjusted the order of candidates top to bottom, to reflect their popularity, as shown in the left-hand shaded column; and the offices have also been re-arranged in descending order of their MBC scores, as shown in the bottom row, left to right.

In many matrix votes analyses, the final outcome when represented in this way will be close to a diagonal, and the closer it is, the more consensual the complete result {In our own example, any proximity to a diagonal is artificial, because four of the office holders' scores (15) and two of the offices' scores (25) are all tied, let alone three and two of their sums in the matrix, (15 and 5)} (Table 4.5).

The above analysis shows what happens if and when there's a tie: priority is first given to the more popular candidate, the one with the higher MBC score, as shown in the right-hand column; if there's still a tie, the appointment goes to the office with the higher MBC score, as shown in the bottom row; if there is still still a tie, even after that, we return to the candidates' scores to see who got the more 1st preferences, or 2nd, or 3rd… and if there is still still still a tie, we'd better all go to the pub.

Table 4.5   The executive committee

MBC	Names	Chair	Secretary	Treasurer	Vice	Press	MBC scores
1st	Veda				5		20
$2^{nd} =$	Eda	15					15
$2^{nd} =$	Fred		15				15
$2^{nd} =$	Freda			15			15
$2^{nd} =$	Ned					5	15
	MBC scores	35	25 =	25 =	20	15	120

4.2.6 The Matrix Vote—Choice

If just one individual chooses an executive, the committee members have no choice. If the AGM elects one person, one at a time, to fill each of the five offices—which is what often happens—every member has a choice of 1 of 8, then 1 of 7, next 1 of 6 and so on, 1 of 5 and 1 of 4, in each of five binary votes. But when they use a matrix vote—ah ha!—each member has a huge choice: any one of 8 to hold any one of 5 offices, followed by any one of 7 to hold any one of 4 posts, and any one of 6 to hold any one of 3, and so on… in all, a choice of some 20,000 different ways of voting. It's also called pluralism (para 2.3.1).

4.3   *Realpolitik*

Life is a little more complicated when a hundred or more members of parliament choose, say, 10 of their colleagues to form the executive. But no matter—all the horrid maths can be done on a computer. Now given that $(10 + 9 + \cdots 1 =) 55$, all of these members will be exercising up to 55 points each, and with so many points flying around, the chances of a tie are much reduced if not minimal. No matter, the rules as described above still apply.

But there might be a few other problems. In the above example, Veda was top, the most popular committee member of all, yet she finished up as the Vice-chair, not the most prestigious of posts perhaps. Some had wanted her to be the Chair, others the Treasurer or Press Officer, and so on.

4.3.1 The Matrix Vote in Stable Democracies

When a parliament is electing a government, there is more at stake: he who aspires to be the prime minister does not want to finish up as the minister of sport, say. Accordingly, instead of a ✓ for 'this' particular candidate to be elected to 'that' particular portfolio, the voting member of parliament may use the letters A, B and C—for each candidate, their three priorities. He gives his top priority candidate an A, for Ms i to be the Minister of Finance for example, and he can also give her a letter B in, say, the Minister of Trade column. If, then, in the count, she is elected to the executive but does not get appointed to the Finance Ministry because someone else got more points for that posting, the points which he gave her as A's in that Finance column will now be transferred and added to her sum in the Trade (her B) column.

The same applies to the voter's letter C, and an example of a completed matrix vote ballot, in this instance for the German Parliament, is shown in Annex VI.

One further refinement should also be stated: in a parliamentary setting, the first analysis, that of the preferences cast in the shaded column, shall best be undertaken by a system of proportional representation PR. As we shall see in the next chapter, some forms of MBC have the advantage that they incentivise the parties to nominate only as many candidates as the parties think can get elected—PR-STV (PR—single transferable vote) and an electoral procedure called the quota Borda system QBS (paras 5.2.9 and 5.2.12). So, if a parliament of say 120 members were electing a cabinet of just 15 ministers, party X with 25% of the parliamentary seats might reasonably expect to win about 25% of the seats in cabinet: i.e. at least three if not four. Party X, therefore, would best be advised to nominate just four candidates, or five at the most, stating with each nomination just which ministerial post they have in mind. If they have more than five candidates, they might split their vote; if they have <4, they might finish up being under-represented. So yes, party X should nominate 5 members. When casting their votes, however, all-party X MPs should best use all 15 preferences. In other words, the matrix vote encourages all members of parliament to vote across the gender gap, the party divide and even the ethno-religious chasm.

This, it is argued, should be an essential feature of any power-sharing structure.

4.3.2   The Matrix Vote in Conflict Zones

Most conflict zones have adopted some form of power-sharing: Northern Ireland's Belfast Agreement devised a system of 'cherry picking', so that all parties in the Assembly could share power in the Executive; Bosnia has a joint presidency of three persons, one from each of the three ethno-religious groups; and Lebanon shares power by distributing executive posts according to the members' confessional beliefs. In other words, all three methodologies tend to perpetuate sectarianism in their systems of power-sharing, if not also in their decision-making, (para 1.4.1).

Further afield, in the wake of the 2007/8 post-election violence, Kenya now enjoys a UN-brokered form of power-sharing. Western advisers were not so successful in Afghanistan, where most of the members of parliament didn't belong to any political party at all,[4] so forming an all-*party* coalition

---

[4] In 2010, the largest party in the *Wolesi Jirga* (parliament) of 249 members had just 17 seats, 18 parties shared 68 seats, and all the other members, all 164 of them, were independents.

was almost impossible. Certain appointments were made on a tribal basis, not unlike the process used in Lebanon, but the Afghan Assembly had the power of veto—a recipe for impasse. Iraq, too, wasted an awful lot of time and political energy when it could ill afford to do so—156 days in 2005—as always arguing about who does what.

The only non-conflict zone to adopt power-sharing is Switzerland. There too, realising that negotiations could be problematic, the parliament adopted a mathematical rule—the 'magic formula' (*Zauberformel*)—so to give the biggest parliamentary parties representation in the seven-person Federal Council. Originally, the rule was 2:2:2:1 for the top four parties in the parliament to share power—2 members each for the three big parties and just 1 for the smaller party—but, with changing political fortunes, this was changed to 2:2:1:1:1 and, so far at least, the magic is working quite well.

Here too, however, the process of forming the executive is based on parties. Given that in many conflict zones, parties tend to be ethno-religious, the Swiss magic if applied in a conflict zone might also perpetuate sectarianism. The matrix vote, in contrast, is colour-blind, and ideally suited to plural societies.

4.4   A Consensual Polity

Accordingly, the democratic process could consist of two elections: the first, an election in which the people choose their representatives, hopefully by PR; the second, which could happen about one week later,[5] could be a PR matrix vote in which the newly elected or re-elected politicians elect their government.

In the latter contest, no-one is a candidate; or rather, every member of parliament is eligible for any ministerial post. A member may opt *out* of any or all portfolios—it's not everyone who would want to be a minister of finance, and some long-serving members of parliament might have already served too long—but nobody opts *in*. Beware the ambitious. Instead, as in a Quaker meeting, only if the consensus wants someone to be an office bearer, should the said individual, no matter how modest, feel obliged to comply.[6]

---

[5] In many countries, the process of appointing an administration can take an age: the world record of 541 days is held by Belgium, in 2010/11. Other nations have also found it difficult—in 2017 Germany took 161 days, the Netherlands in 2021, 298! The matrix vote could ensure that everything is done fairly... and quickly!

[6] In 1598, Boris Godunov was dragged to the Russian throne, supposedly reluctantly, while in a similar manner, the tradition in China was for a newly chosen emperor to politely refuse, three times.

No longer would the appointment of ministers be at the whim or will of just the one prime minister or president. And if, at some later stage, a minister is unable to continue in post—being in prison, a hospital or a graveyard—the ballots may simply be re-counted with this particular member now removed from the analysis. Needless to say, any such recount will still be proportional, and the consequent re-shuffle will probably affect only two or three ministers.

4.4.1 Consensus for the Non-consensual

In theory and in practice, especially with a PR election, some of the members elected to parliament might be extremists. Then, with a PR matrix vote, some of them might get elected to government. (In contrast, if parliament is majoritarian, the danger is that an extremist once elected might then dominate... as did Hitler.)

A consensus polity recognises the fact that a society might have its extremists and, if so, that they should be represented in their proportional due. Better the camel in the tent pissing out, as they say, than outside pissing in. The hope is, of course, that when confronted with the responsibilities of governance, the extremists will moderate their behaviour. If they don't, if they just piss around, then come the next election, the electorate will surely tell them to piss off. (End of metaphor.) That is the democratic hope.

The executive shall work in consensus. The extremist might find this difficult. Indeed, the resulting failure to get any of his extremist policies adopted might be altogether just too frustrating. So he might well moderate his ways. Or resign. In general, it is probably fair to conclude that narcissists like Donald Trump would not find consensus easy: being allowed to speak only so many times, and even then for only so many minutes; using preference voting such that, if he states only his 1st preference, his influence on the outcome would be minimal; holding office on a shared basis, rotating posts, each of which has a deputy from another party; sharing responsibility for implementing those decisions for which there is a consensus... no, in such a setting, he wouldn't last long.

4.4.2 Choice

We might also note that, when a parliament of 100 elects an executive of 10, there are 100 × 10 ways in which each may cast a 1st preference, 99 × 9 for the 2nd preference, and so on; in all, every member shall have a choice of some 300 million trillion ways of completing his matrix vote ballot. That's not just pluralism; that's freedom, freedom of choice. And if the members of parliament enjoy such a huge degree of choice, the chances of any one leader being able to 'democratically dictate' who does what would be just about nil. There again, by definition, a democracy should never be top-down.

4.5   Conclusion

Majority rule, the domination of one faction over the other(s), has often caused dysfunction in some governments; at worst, it has provoked violence and war. Admittedly, there are some who baulk at the idea of having to share power with extremists. But extremists are only attracted to power if that power is exercised by (force or) majority vote.

Hitler, Stalin[7] and Máo would probably not have won power if such had depended on their electorate's use of a sophisticated electoral system; and they would not have survived, politically, if all non-urgent decisions taken were only those which received a minimum degree of consensus support. It's time we had a look at the world's various electoral systems.

Reference

Arrow, K. J. (1963). *Social choice and individual values*. New Haven and London: Yale University Press.

---

[7] The Bolsheviks ('members of the majority') did actually hold one election, the very purpose of which was to show that they *were* the majority... and they lost! This was in November 1917, just after the so-called October Revolution, and the Bolsheviks won <25%! Of 707 deputies, the Socialist Revolutionaries had 370—an absolute majority—while the Bolsheviks got only 175 and the Mensheviks a mere 16. Lenin therefore sent in 'the boys' and the Constituent Assembly was prorogued. The rest is horrible history.

5

'The People Have Voted... The [Expletives]!'*—Comparing Electoral Systems

It's not the people who vote that count,
It's the people who count the votes.

Jozef Stalin

Abstract In a representative democracy, a fair political structure can only materialise if, first and foremost, both the electoral system and the decision-making system are themselves fair. Some electoral systems, though often used, are most definitely unfair. Others, less frequently seen, are mediocre. A few, rarely employed, are excellent. And one, which most people have never even heard of, is robust, proportional, preferential, accurate, inclusive... and very democratic: the Quota Borda System, QBS.

Keywords Inclusive politics · Compromise · Preferential proportional voting · Quota Borda System QBS · Elections

---

*I quote a candidate in a Belfast City Council election. At an early stage of the count, he thought he had lost, and hence this utterance... but he then went on to be successfully elected! He in turn was quoting Dick Tuck, who thus introduced his concession speech in 1966 having failed in his bid for the California State Senate.

P. Emerson, *The Punters' Guide to Democracy*,
https://doi.org/10.1007/978-3-031-06987-1_5

5.1   Introduction

In decision-making, as we saw in Chaps. 3 and 4, compromise can be achieved both in debate and in the vote, and sometimes too in the analysis. When it comes to an election however... well, you can't tweak or amend let alone composite a candidate, and you certainly shouldn't delete any of them.[1] But we can ensure a degree of compromise with PR, that is, by allowing for more than one winner.

Accordingly, we should never elect only one individual—one president, one prime minister, one chairperson, whatever. At the very least, we should always elect at least two persons—the boss and a deputy, for example; better still, in a general election, we could elect, say, a full half a dozen representatives in what are called multi-member constituencies—or even the entire parliament in just the one constituency, the whole country; next, at best, the elected representatives could use a matrix vote to elect their executive, for that would guarantee compromise.

5.2   A Choice of Electoral Systems

So now comes the question of which electoral system should best be used? There are many to choose from, over 300 of them, and nearly every system is regarded by some if not by all as democratic. (There are also quite a few ways of making decisions, as we saw in Chap. 2, but while we only ever make one decision or one prioritisation in decision-making, an election, as we've just noted, may sometimes elect more than one person, and sometimes proportionally. So there are indeed rather more electoral systems than there are decision-making systems).

That said, it is still odd that many politicians and others act as if there is only one decision-making voting system which is truly democratic—the very one that isn't very democratic at all, the (simple or weighted) majority vote; at the same time, they often imply that lots of electoral systems are just fine, and that every country may regard the one they have chosen as a perfectly understandable matter of individual national choice.

Some go on to say, and here they are joined by many academics, that nothing's perfect[2]... which may be true, so to imply that something imperfect may nevertheless be OK. Of the world's many electoral systems, however—as

---

[1] In some Russian elections, voters were allowed to delete—'*vycherknut*' вычеркнуть—a candidate, to 'cross out' his/her name... which always sounded a bit Stalinist to me.

[2] Kenneth Arrow's Impossibility Theorem, (para 6.4.1).

we shall now see—some are distinctly unfair, others are just about adequate, while only a few are inclusive and accurate... and a couple almost perfect.

To judge them all is not easy, but we'll try. And maybe a good way of doing so is to compare an election with a sporting event: in the latter, we want to find out who is the best athlete or which is the best team, and in the former we try to see who is/are the most popular candidate(s); in all such contests, certain rules apply, the very purpose of which should be to uphold fairness.[3] But first, let's look at a few details which apply to any country's electoral system.

Any system which allows the voters to cast only one preference is inadequate. It's as if, in casting his vote, the voter is declaring: '"this" candidate good, "that" or "those" candidate(s) bad', so it too is Orwellian and primitive. Basically, a voter cannot express her opinion on a list of candidates *accurately* if she is able to express a view only on one of them. And if the individual vote is not accurate, then the analysis, the collation of a lot of inaccurate data, will in all probability itself be inaccurate. Thirdly, as we stated earlier, elections should nearly always be for more than one representative, so instead of a very large number of single-seat constituencies (as in Britain), there could be a smaller number of multi-member constituencies (as in Ireland) or even just one big constituency (as in Israel, the Netherlands and Ukraine).

5.2.1 The Binary Ballot

So now let's look at the various electoral systems. The worst of all is the simple binary 'Candidate X, yes or no?' type of election. As we mentioned, it was used by Napoléon in his third referendum of 1803, and thus he became the emperor (para 1.1). It was also used in Georgia in 1992 to elect Eduard Shevardnadze as the first President of Georgia, but that was during a civil war. And this simplistic system is used today in North Korea. Basically—and it is pretty basic—the party, the only party, chooses the candidate, the only candidate, and the people then vote 'yes' or 'no'... (or maybe just 'yes' or 'yes').

---

[3] I have been an election observer in over 20 elections, usually for the Organisation for Security and Co-operation in Europe, OSCE. The purpose of any election observation mission is to judge whether or not an election is 'free and fair'. The phrase implies that the state should be neutral; that campaigning candidates should be treated equally, not least by the press; and that voters should be able to go to the polling station to cast their ballot, without fear of intimidation or violence. Alas, these missions seldom if ever comment on the fairness or otherwise of the electoral system.

There is no competition, so there's no sporting analogy, but it can be compared to our (western) decision-making voting system in its parliamentary setting, (paras 1.1 and 1.2), especially in a two-party state whenever members of Congress (in the US) or Parliament (in the UK) vote 'yes' or 'yes' if they belong to the ruling party, and 'no' or 'no' if they belong to the opposition… and on either side, if they don't do as they are told to do, they may well lose the whip, (para 4.1), the chance of a ministerial career, or even their parliamentary seat come the next election! So we'll dismiss North Korea's binary electoral system, just as we dismissed our binary decision-making, and move on to the next one.

5.2.2   First-Past-The-Post

A slightly better methodology, first-past-the-post FPTP, is the same as plurality voting in decision-making, (para 2.2.1). There may be just two, or maybe lots of candidates, but the voter is able to choose only one of them— 'this' one good… and here we go again; FPTP is also Orwellian. Yes, it is primitive, very adversarial, and cannot accurately reflect the punter's viewpoint. But it is used in the UK, the USA, Canada, India, many other nations of the former British Empire, and quite a few autocratic democrats also favour this crude methodology.

One further disadvantage is this: as the late Michael Dummett wrote, "There is no post," (Dummett, 1997: 39). In a two-candidate contest, the winner will need 50% + 1 of the vote. If there are three candidates, success might come in at 33% + 1; the quota, as it is called. If there are four, victory could be achieved on just 25% + 1. And so on… so with 20 candidates or more, well, in theory, you could get into parliament on just 5% of the vote; everybody else, all 95% of the voters, might think you're the worst of all, but if none of the other candidates gets more than 4.9%, then sure enough, 5% can seal the win. This actually happened in Papua New Guinea PNG, so the good people of the former British colony then decided to ditch the ol' British FPTP and to adopt a better, preferential system (see para 5.2.5), which the good people of Britain refused in a (ridiculous, binary) referendum in 2011.[4]

---

[4] New Zealand had a choice of FPTP and four other systems, (para 3.2.1, Footnote 3). Britain was given only a binary ballot: FPTP versus a preferential but not proportional system (para 5.2.5); so neither was PR. For any PR supporter, therefore, the referendum question was like that of the waiter who asks the vegetarian, 'beef or lamb?' Everyone seems to understand this, it seems, except the UK's Electoral Commission.

The obvious sporting analogy is the horse race, the difference being that the 'post' is moved back towards the starting line, every time another horse enters the turnstiles until, when there are 20 or more of them, the finish is only a metre or two from the starting line.

A further disadvantage is that, in politics, there should be no favourites; alas, in politics, not least because of the media, all the money is often on only two of the candidates, if not indeed on just one of them.

FPTP is sometimes hopelessly unfair. In Ethiopia for example in 2015, nearly 2,000 candidates of over 40 parties competed... but every single seat was won by just the one-party or its ally. Sometimes, however, it's not too bad. In Lebanon, for its Taif Accords of 1943 (when there were no western experts, the latter were all too busy, fighting a war), the Lebanese devised a variation of FPTP which remains imperfect but brilliant. A constituency of, say, 50% Druze, 25% Maronite and 25% Sunni, shall elect 4 candidates (if it's a small constituency) or a multiple of 4 (if it's a big constituency). Any party may stand, but their 4× candidates must all be in that same 2:1:1 ratio of confessional belief. In theory, then, every political party is non-sectarian; (would that the system in Northern Ireland had had such a feature).

Dagestan also had a pretty cute answer to the problem. The country was divided into so many constituencies, and each one was designated as of one ethno-religious group; then, come the election, every candidate of every party had to belong to that grouping. So again, in theory, sectarianism played no part in politics. In theory. Alas, in 2007, they adopted a PR-list system but, by all accounts, the problems have not eased.

5.2.3   The Two-Round System

The Two-round System TRS was discussed in para 2.2.2, and because it is based on the potentially inaccurate plurality vote, it too can be hopelessly unfair. At best (or worst), TRS only encourages more horses to join in the race (or fray).

The British gave many of their former colonies FPTP, and in a similar fashion, France bequeathed TRS to many of hers.

5.2.4   Serial Voting

Serial voting (para 2.2.4) requires all the options to be laid out on a spectrum, from small to large, from left-wing to right-, whatever. But you can't put candidates into some sort of linear spectrum—the Greens for one would object—so serial voting, often used in Scandinavia for decision-making, is not regarded as an electoral system.

The best sporting analogy for any of three knock-out systems—TRS, serial voting and the next one, AV—is probably a tennis tournament, but the latter only works well if the players are seeded. Otherwise, in a competition of eight players, for instance, you might finish up with a final, not between the two best players, but between the best and the 5th best. Secondly, just as you can't tweak, amend, composite or categorise candidates, you shouldn't try to seed them either. We move on.

5.2.5   The Alternative Vote

As we mentioned in para 2.2.3, the Alternative Vote AV is preferential. The voter votes 1, 2, 3… for as many candidates as she wants. In the count, if no-one candidate has received a majority of the 1st preferences, the least popular is eliminated and his votes are transferred, in accordance with his voters' 2nd preferences. The process continues until one candidate gains a majority. So AV caters for a less adversarial contest. Indeed, success for any one candidate may often depend on the 2nd and/or subsequent preferences from other candidates, so in many election campaigns, as seen in Australia, at least some candidates will be incentivised to cooperate.

PNG (para 5.2.2) has gone one stage further, for they now use AV, with one additional proviso: a vote is valid only if it includes three preferences. With FPTP, with one candidate for 'this' tribe, and another for 'that', elections were often very tribal; furthermore, there were sometimes 20 or more 'thises' and 'that's', every candidate of a different tribe, and many voters voted on these tribal lines. Now, however, with the requirement of at least three preferences, voters are encouraged to cross the tribal divide. Again, Northern Ireland has much to learn.

5.2.6   Approval Voting

Approval Voting (para 2.2.5) is meant to be a gentler sport. Unfortunately, however, voters who support more than one player and who are thus prepared to compromise may well thereby reduce the chances of their favourite. And vice versa: those with the vice of intransigence are more likely to succeed. It is not used in any national elections, but it is deployed in the one-party or no-party village council elections in China, and often fairly successfully.

5.2.7   Range Voting

Range voting (para 2.2.6) is also not used nationally. It can best be compared, not to a sport, but to a rutting contest. The stags fight to mate. While all the consensual stags are engaged in open combat, horns locked in fierce but fair contest, the unconsensual by-stander can put all their strength into a thrust of their horns into a competing contestant's under-belly. It's not the best parallel, but range voting does encourage the voter to be utterly selfish.

5.2.8   Some Other PR Systems

PR comes in quite a few different formats. The simplest, a closed-list system as in Israel, allows the voter to choose just one-party; so it's not a little Orwellian and rather like a horse race. The open list system gives the voter a little more choice, and he can now choose either just a party or, if he so desires, one particular candidate from the party of his choice, as in Bosnia and the Netherlands. Better still is the Belgian version, which allows the voter to vote for more than one candidate, as long as they all come from the one-party. And the best of all these systems, the Swiss version, gives the voter the chance to support candidates of more than one-party—to cross the gender and/or party and/or even the sectarian divides... if she wants to.

One disadvantage of the PR-list systems is that proportionality is defined by the party labels. In contrast, with the more sophisticated PR-STV and QBS, (paras 5.2.9 and 5.2.12), proportionality is defined by the voters themselves... and if a quota of voters gives a 1st preference to candidate X because of her gender, for example, then sure enough, she will be elected.

A sporting equivalent could perhaps be the marathon in which many an athlete thinks finishing is more important than winning. Likewise, in a six-seater PR election, the six winning candidates will all hold the same status—they all finished the course—and it matters not, who came in first and who sixth.

5.2.9   Proportional Representation—Single Transferable Vote

PR-STV is AV in multi-member constituencies, so to be successful, a candidate needs, not 50% + 1, (para 5.2.2), but only a smaller quota; in a four-seater constituency, that could be just 20% + 1.

In the count, any candidate with a quota of 1st preferences is elected. If any of them has more than a quota, her surplus is transferred in accordance with her voters' 2nd preferences, usually in proportion; so if 10% of candidate X's 2nd preferences went to candidate Y, and candidate X was elected, Y would receive 10% of the surplus: hence all those decimal points. More simple are the transfers from any candidate eliminated because of a very low score, where whole numbers survive.

As we implied when discussing the matrix vote, (para 4.3.1), PR-STV has the added advantage that it inherently encourages every party to nominate only as many candidates as it thinks it can get elected. If it has, say, 30% support in any one constituency, and if the quota is, oh, 12%, then it should get two or maybe three candidates elected. If unwisely it nominates five candidates, each might get the support of only 6% or half a quota, so maybe none will get elected, not at the first stage anyway.

A disadvantage of PR-STV lies in the fact that the candidate who gets a very low 1st preference score but a good number of 2nd preferences—in other words, the perfect compromise candidate—might get eliminated in stage (i) of the count, and may never know of all those 2nd preferences, rather like option D in Table 1.1. PR-STV[5] is used in Ireland,[6] Malta and Tasmania.

The best sporting analogy for PR-STV is probably a game of bowls where victory amongst the big players might well depend upon the strike of just one small contestant, whose transfer of votes can aid one bowl substantially, and knock another leading contestant completely out of contention.[7] So PR-STV is a very good system, but it can be capricious.

5.2.10   The Borda and Condorcet Rules

Two preferential systems—the modified Borda count MBC and Condorcet—were seen to be the fairest decision-making methodologies (paras 2.2.7 and 2.2.8), so maybe they too could form the basis of very good electoral systems.

---

[5] In the count of one PR-STV local council election in Belfast, the returning officer told me I was the best compromise candidate of all, with 2nd and/or 3rd preferences from right-across the spectrum, but I was eliminated at a fairly early stage, so most of these preferences were never even counted.

[6] PR-STV was imposed on the Irish, North and South, as part of the 1920 Settlement. The hope was that, as a result, some Catholics would be elected in the North, some Protestants in the South, and after a week or two, everyone would fall in love again. Up North, the Unionists just scrapped it. Down South, the constitution stipulated that any such change required a referendum... and while many Irish politicians didn't like this British invention of PR-STV and preferred the British FPTP, the people said 'no', once in 1959 by 52% on a 58% turnout, and on the second occasion in 1968 on a 66% turnout with a much bigger (Ulster-style) 'NO!' of 61%.

[7] The technical term is monotonicity, and it's in the Glossary.

Perhaps the fairest of all sporting competitions is a league system, as happens in many football tournaments. Let every team play every other team, and then let's see either which team wins the most matches and/or which scores the most goals.

In both the MBC and Condorcet, the voters cast their preferences. Next, in an MBC count, we add up all the points (or goals) to see which candidates score the most points (or have the best goal difference)—the Borda rule; or we compare the candidates in pairs—**A/B, A/C** etc.—just as we did in decision-making (para 1.1), to see which candidate wins the most pairings (or matches), and that's a Condorcet winner.

Now in most football competitions, the champion—the winner of the league, the team which wins the most matches—is also the team with the best goal difference. Likewise in politics: the option or candidate which/who wins the most pairings—the Condorcet winner—is often, also, the option or candidate which/who scores the most points—the MBC social choice. Which is why we concluded in para 2.6 that the best form of decision-making, the one which should be used in any nation's supreme decision-making chamber, is the combined MBC/Condorcet count.

The BC is used in elections in Slovenia, albeit just for the election of ethnic-minority representatives. The Condorcet rule is not used in national elections (para 5.2.13).

5.2.11   A Two-Tier Electoral System

A further variation on the theme of electoral systems is a two-tier system. In Germany and New Zealand, for example, the voter is given two ballots: the first is for an FPTP election which is held in lots of small constituencies, which means, in many instances, the successful candidate is a local; the second is a PR-list election held in the larger regional constituencies, the Länder. What's more, the PR 'half' determines the ratio of parties in the Bundestag, but no-one elected shall be unelected; instead, the party with a good PR result will get a few extra seats.

In other two-tier systems, the PR bit does not affect the overall result. In Russia, for example, it's 50:50, whereas in Taiwan, two-thirds are elected under the very unproportional FPTP, and only one third under PR, so the system is at best only semi-PR.

A sporting analogy is a little more difficult, unless we say it's a game of two 'halves'. Suffice to say that while FPTP tends to produce a two-party structure with two big parties, and PR often leads to a multi-party structure with lots of parties, big, average and small; so the German electoral system of multi-member proportional MMP, which is half-and-half—50% of the MPs are elected under FPTP, and 50% by PR, roughly—and this often produces a *Bundestag* (parliament) of two big parties and a few little ones.

5.2.12   The Quota Borda System

Now the MBC is not proportional, so Professor Sir Michael Dummett added a quota to create a new voting procedure, the Quota Borda System QBS (Dummett, 1997: 151–7; Emerson, 2020: 62–70). Candidates compete in multi-member constituencies; the voters cast their preferences—in a six-seater constituency, the recommended number of preferences for a full ballot is six—and the count is conducted in several stages, as follows; to take a simple version:

stage (i) all candidates with a quota of 1st preferences are elected;
stage (ii) all pairs of candidates[8] with two quotas are elected;
and, if seats are still to be filled:
stage (iii) the remaining seats go to those as yet unelected candidates with the highest MBC scores.

5.2.13   Condorcet

Condorcet could be used as an electoral system, especially if the count was an electronic one. The complications of sorting out pairs, however, especially when there are 20 (or more) candidates, which would involve 210 (or more) pairings, has meant that it's use is more confined to decision-making.

5.3   An Overview

Now let's look at the practical implications. In binary voting and FPTP, some voters vote not so much 'for' their 1st preference candidate, more 'against' their last preference. Both systems are very adversarial and, as often as not,

---

[8] What is a QBS pair? OK, let's take a hypothetical example from Northern Ireland: the Rev Ian Paisley and his son. If daddy and sonny-boy were both standing in the same constituency, lots of voters might vote 1st–2nd for dad-son, and a few might vote 1st–2nd for son-dad. In stage (i) of the count, if daddy has a quota of 1st preferences, he gets elected, while sonny with less than a quota remains as yet unelected.

In stage (ii), if daddy's 1st–2nd (dad-son) vote plus sonny's 1st–2nd (son-dad) vote is more than two quotas, then the dad-son pair has qualified, and sonny gets elected as well. (Altogether much easier than transferring surpluses with decimal points and other additional complications… as in PR-STV.).

the candidates use adversarial language: they *fight* elections and hope to *defeat* their opponents—it is all the language of war.

Some PR systems and even PR-STV also suffer from this weakness, and there are those candidates, especially those who reckon they already have a quota or more of support, who sometimes try to bolster their support from amongst their supporters by antagonising their opponents.

But not with QBS. As was noted (para 4.3.1), QBS (like PR-STV) prompts every party to nominate only as many candidates as it thinks it can get elected. Furthermore, because it is based on the MBC, QBS (unlike PR-STV) encourages the voters to submit a full ballot.

Let's take a very simple example from a really complex setting—Bosnia-Herzegovina. Consider a six-seater constituency in which the population is split 30:30:30, Muslim: Orthodox: Catholic. Given that ratio, each sectarian grouping can hope to get two candidates elected; given a degree of optimism, a non-sectarian party like the Socialists might also have a go. Now because so many people in countries, societies and parties, believe in majority voting, many sectarian groups themselves tend to split into two major parties, the one more extreme than its rival, though there may also be one or two little parties, fractious fractions of the whole. But with QBS, maybe they should cooperate, lest they split the vote and lose everything. The incentive, then, is for each political and/or sectarian grouping to nominate only two or at most three candidates; so maybe the ballot paper will list just 10 or 12 candidates, 3 of each from the three sectarian groups, and one or two from the non-sectarian sector.

In voting in a six-seater QBS constituency, every voter shall be entitled to, and well advised to, cast all six preferences; but maybe there are only three candidates of his ethno-religious group. So he is encouraged to cross the party divide if not indeed the sectarian chasm.[9] So the voter casts his preferences, not only for those of 'his own'. In so doing, he recognises the validity of these fellow citizens to their candidacies, and acknowledges the fact that the outcome will be a mix, all elected in proportion to their electoral support.

In a word, QBS is brilliant. Which maybe explains why it is not used anywhere. Not yet.

---

[9] PR-STV *allows* the voters to cross the divides but, as seen in Northern Ireland, many supporters of the more extreme parties do not; in contrast, QBS actually *encourages* them to do so.

5.4   Conclusion

That's not the full survey of all 300 + electoral systems, but a fair sample of them. Maybe we should put them into a table to compare them all—all, that is, except range voting—as in Table 5.1.

Democracy is often regarded as a prerequisite of any peace settlement, but if peace is to be achieved, the voting procedures used in any post-conflict settlement should themselves be 'peaceful'. Many divided societies have adopted a proportional electoral system—Northern Ireland has retained its PR-STV; Bosnia has adopted PR-list; while Lebanon has devised a good

Table 5.1 Voting procedures—a comparison

		VOTING PROCEDURES		
		DECISION-MAKING	ELECTIONS	
		BINARY CHOICE		
Majority voting	Every-where	Option X, yes or no?	Candidate X, yes or no?	DPRK
		Option X or option Y	Candidate X or Y?	USA
		MULTIPLE CHOICE		
Only 1st preferences	Denmark	Plurality voting	FPTP	UK / India
			PR-list	Belgium / Swiss
			TRS + PR-list = Parallel[1]	Japan / Russia
			MBC + PR-list = MMP	Germany / NZ
Knock-out systems	NZ	TRS		France
		AV, IRV, PV, RCV or STV		Australia
			Single transferable vote PR-STV	Ireland / Malta
	Sweden	Serial voting		
Non-preferential		Approval voting		China[2]
Preferential		BC		Nauru[3] / Slovenia
		MBC		
			QBS	
		Condorcet		

[1] The PR part has no bearing on the other, whereas, in MMP, it does (para 5.2.11).
[2] Chinese villages normally elect their Village Councils every three years.
[3] Nauru uses a unique system: a 1st preference gets 1 point, a 2nd gets ½... a 4th ¼... etc., which is only brilliant.

(but imperfect) non-sectarian form of FPTP (para 5.2.2)—but few if any have chosen a fair decision-making system. At best, they have opted for a twin majority system, the so-called consociational vote (para 7.2.1), but the latter is still binary.

One other observation deserves a mention. The powers that be—for Northern Ireland and Bosnia, the US and UK both played a major part, (as did Ireland of course in the former conflict)—often advocate a very good electoral system for those affected, but both the US and UK have failed to apply the same peaceful criteria for their own populations. Likewise, all three 'stable democracies' advocate a form of consociational decision-making and all-party power-sharing for these conflict zones... but never for themselves.

References

Dummett, M. (1997). *Principles of electoral reform*, Oxford University Press, Oxford.
Emerson, P. (2020). *Democratic decision-making*, Springer, Heidelberg.

6

A Little Long History of Voting Systems

In the history of democratic thought, the past has a huge presence, a history that is both inspirational and instructive in the contemporary world.
Amartya Sen, *Home in the World*, p. 109.

Abstract Maybe they got it wrong. Maybe, when the European powers became such an influence in the world and acquired the habit of preaching their ideas to, and imposing these ideas on, all and sundry, maybe they made a mistake or two. Indeed, maybe some of the other civilisations had better ideals. One such belief might be that no majority has the democratic right to dominate a minority; instead, all should seek the common good. From ages past, many have been those who have campaigned for this democratic ideal. The seeds have often been sown. Sometimes the plants have grown. Rarely have they been harvested.

Keywords Social choice science · Preferential voting · Demos · Consensus · Pluralism · Referendums · Modified Borda count

6.1 Introduction

In years gone by, decision-making was often binary and violent, and disputes were often 'resolved' by force of arms. Many still are. One of the first improvements was the device called majority voting. It was still binary, of course, but matters could now be decided by force of numbers.

© The Author(s), under exclusive license to Springer Nature
Switzerland AG 2022
P. Emerson, *The Punters' Guide to Democracy*,
https://doi.org/10.1007/978-3-031-06987-1_6

6.2   Traditional Structures

Societies everywhere have devised their own forms of collective decision-making. In the Americas, the native peoples sat in circles, shared a pipe, and sorted everything out in a pow-wow. Africans also sat down, usually under a tree—after all, it was more comfortable to sit on grass and in the shade, rather than on dried earth in the glare of the sun—indeed, the very word for such a get-together, in Rwanda, is *gacaca*, whose original meaning is 'grass'. While in Europe and in Asia, almost everywhere, it seems, peoples met in circles and came to collective decisions, without voting. We start where homo sapiens started, in Africa.

6.2.1   Africa

Throughout sub-Saharan Africa, "Majority rule was a foreign notion. [Our] democracy meant all [people] were to be heard, and a decision was taken together as a people. A minority was not to be crushed by a majority." (Mandela, 1994: 25). Accordingly, as embodied in words like *baraza*—the Kiswahili equivalent of *gacaca*—democracy was always regarded as an inclusive process; "The elders sit under the big tree," as President Julius Nyerere of Tanzania once wrote, "and talk until they agree" (Sigmund, 1966: 197). Admittedly, the process might be protracted; never mind, if they couldn't get consensus today, all would be postponed until the morrow, when they'd try again.

In like manner, African courts of law were sometimes far less adversarial than their European equivalents. In Ethiopia in former years (but we switch to the present tense), "… conflicts and disputes are jointly resolved. If someone in the village is quarrelling with someone else, then the court convened beneath the tree… will set itself the sole task of ending the conflict and conciliating the warring sides, while granting to each that he is in the right" (Kapuściński, 2001: 315).

Sadly, the European powers tended to dislike this 'consensus nonsense'—generally speaking, the European does not have the patience of the African—and majority voting was imposed on the former colonies when the latter received their independence. But was it right, we may ask if only in retrospect, to impose majority rule on Rwanda? Or Kenya? Or anywhere?

6.2.2 Asia

Asia's next. Now many people think that China is full of Chinese, and we tend to forget that in years long gone, this huge land mass was inhabited by many different peoples—not just the Hàn, but the Tangut (Dǎngxiàng), Xiōngnú and so on. Meanwhile, to the north and on the far side of the Great Wall, there were the other peoples (whom the Chinese used to call barbarians)—not least the Khitans[1] (Qìdān), Jurchens (Nǔzhēn) and Mongolians—all of whom at one stage or another crossed that wall and ruled huge parts of China; indeed, the Mongolians conquered all of it in what became the Yuán Dynasty.

The first, the Khitans' Liáo Dynasty, was from 916 to 1125; the Jurchens' Jīn Dynasty came next, followed by the Mongols in 1234. All of these peoples had "as a part of their heritage of their tribal past a strong tradition of deliberation and joint decision-making" (Franke & Twitchett, 1994: 24). It was not unlike what was happening in Scandinavia a thousand odd years ago, by the sound of *Tings*: 'ting' is a Norwegian word which means 'assembly'[2] and at a "meeting of the Ting the freemen settled disputes; discussed, accepted and rejected laws... and even elected or gave their approval to a king—who was often required to swear his faithfulness to [those laws]" (Dahl, 1998: 18).

But we go back to Asia and, firstly, the Khitans, where, "Every three years the chieftains of the eight tribes gathered together, to elect (or confirm in his office) one of their number to serve as khagan... [His] tenure of office was not for life; he might be removed from his office and replaced" (Franke & Twitchett, 1994: 52). Then, "Twice a year... the emperor summoned all the executive heads of his government into assembly... These 'great conferences'... decided policy, received nominations for offices, and reviewed all the work of government" (Mote, 2015: 89).

In like manner, to take the second group of 'barbarians', "The tribal election of rulers had been practiced for a long time amongst the Jurchens," and anyone could be chosen, as long as he was a member of the leading tribe (Franke & Twitchett, 1994: 221). Maybe the best example of their democratic beginnings lies in this quotation:

> When their country is involved in great affairs [war], they all go out into the wilderness and sit down in a circle, drawing in the ashes. Then they deliberate, starting from the lowest one present.

---

[1] Which explains why the Russian word for 'China' is *Kitai*, Китай.

[2] It also means 'thing'.

When the council has come to an end… not a human voice is heard. When the army is about to march, a great reunion with a banquet is held, at which strategic proposals are offered.

When the army returns after a victory, another great reunion takes place, and it is asked who has won merits. According to the degree of merit, gold is handed out; it is raised and shown to the multitude. If they think the reward too small, it will be increased." (*Ibid*: 226.)

It is all part of what the *Cambridge History of China* calls a "military democracy", (*ibid*: 24).

The third example relates to "the typical Mongol tribal government spirit of consultation and consensus… They held meetings (endless and too numerous, the Chinese sometimes complained),[3] discussed options, and often exerted their influence reasonably, seeking agreement with the entire staff of officials… perhaps even to the extent of lacking decisiveness" (Mote, 2015: 493).

6.2.3   Europe, Demos and the World

Europe was different. Force of numbers was definitely better than force of arms, and hence the democracy of the City States, starting in Greece with the Solon Constitution in the 6th Century BCE. Demos, the people—well, the males… well, the rich males—went down to the forum, discussed the issues of the day, and took decisions by majority vote; these were then executed by the executive. The crucial thing was the decision; of far less importance were the particular persons of the executive, the mere functionaries, so these were chosen by lot, not least because, "It was believed that the gods designated the most worthy by making his name jump out of the urn" (De Ste Croix, 2005: 95).

On decision-making, however, the Gods were seemingly not to be trusted, and the Ancient Greeks relied more on themselves. But my word, they knew their onions. They

…learned by example (the surest method of instruction) the powers of the proposer, the rights of expressing an opinion, the authority of office holders, and the privileges of ordinary members; they learned when to give way and

---

[3] In a similar fashion, as noted above, the Europeans complained about the Africans' tendency to talk and talk… and talk… in their circles, their *barazas* and *gacacas*; the difference being, of course, that while the Europeans were the colonisers, the Chinese were the colonised.

when to stand firm, how long to speak and when to keep silence, how to distin-
guish between conflicting proposals and how to introduce an amendment, in
short the whole of senatorial procedure.

This is Pliny the Younger, writing in the year 105, (McLean & Urken,
1995: 67). In other words, they understood the truism we quoted in para
1.3: "when there's no majority in favour of any one option, then, obviously,
there's a majority against every option." They therefore devised those very
binary procedures, the ones that we still use today, not least because, in those
days long gone, binary voting was the only decision-making voting procedure
that had yet been devised. {For the first improvement, plurality voting (para
2.2.1), credit goes to the same Pliny the Younger.}

Interestingly, the Chinese also used binary voting in decision-making, and
as far as I know, the earliest known ballot was in the year 61 BCE, a vote
which was won "with a majority of 80%" (Wang, 1968: 176–7). Admittedly,
the electorate was again all male, and definitely all relatively rich—ministers in the Imperial Court—but history relates that the emperor usually went
along with whatever a majority of his ministers had voted for.

Something, however, was not quite right, binary voting had its limitations,
and Pliny the Younger was the first (I think) to write that binary voting is fine
if and when there are only two options on the table. This might be the case
in a court of law—guilty or not guilty?—but as we said in para 2.1, it should
not be the case in any contemporary political controversy. The incident he
quoted, however, was actually from a court of law in the year 105. The
Consul, Afranius Dexter, had been murdered! His manservants lay accused,
and the jury was faced with three options: *A* acquittal, *B* banishment, and *C*
capital punishment.

Pliny realised that if the jury was asked a binary question like 'Are the
accused innocent, yes or no?' the *B* and *C* supporters would gang up against
those of *A*. Or if asked, 'Execution, yes or no?' the *A* and *B* folks would join
forces against *C*. And so on. Suffice here to say that the story finished on a
compromise, and the accused were allowed to live out their days, option *B*,
(which is what Pliny had wanted).

Others also became aware of the limitations of binary voting, and we
return to China where, in 1197, even though the question was binary—
"...whether or not the Mongols should be attacked."—the ballot was
multi-optional. "A vote was taken amongst the highest officials, and... out of
84, only 5 favoured an attack, 46 were for a defensive strategy, and the rest
[33] preferred alternating between attack and defence" (Franke & Twitchett,
1994: 266). It was, then, a plurality vote—the world's first, I reckon, the first
to be taken at a governmental level—and happily, the pacifist option came
out on top.

Not so happily, the effect was short lived. Chinggis Khan was elected in a *Khuriltai*—a Mongolian 'ting'—in 1206, and the rest, as they say, is yet more horrible history. The Jīn Dynasty collapsed in 1234, so that was the end of Jurchen rule, and Chinggis Khan's grandson, Khubilai Khan, went on to conquer, not the entire world as grandpa had wanted, just all of China. Sadly, like the Jurchen emperors before him, he rather liked the authoritarianism of previous Chinese rulers, those of the Sòng and earlier dynasties, and all the democratic traditions of the Jurchens and the Mongols followed those of the Khitans into the history books—(well, a few historical tomes; none of these peoples got even a mention in any of the literary works in my school library).

6.3   From Binary Voting to Pluralism

The above multi-option vote of 1197 is definitely worth a mention. Doubtless it emerged as a possible way of decision-making because of the Jurchens' customs and traditions. Prior to the founding of the Jīn Dynasty, the Jurchen had "no name for their state." In those times, they lived "scattered in the mountains and valleys and elect[ed] for themselves a brave and valiant person as chieftain" (*Ibid*: 265). Pluralism and multi-option voting, I suspect, were just the obvious consequences. And hence too, perhaps, the Chinese words, 圆坐 *yuán zuò* and 圆议 *yuán yì*, 'to sit in circles and discuss'.

At about the same time, Europe was beginning to come out of the Dark Ages, and here too, circles had been the obvious format—as with England's King Arthur and his famous round table.[4] Now in Ancient Greece, discussions had centred on decision-making, whereas later on, people concentrated more on electoral systems. Political questions throughout those days (and today) were invariably regarded as binary, but elections for the papacy and so on, often offered a choice of many more than just two candidates, and three "concepts of modern voting theory—the Borda rule, the Condorcet principle and approval voting—[were] in use in medieval Europe" (McLean & Urken, 1995: 22).

On decision-making, everyone knew that unanimity seldom exists, not in politics. They realised full well that minority rule was not good. And not least Jeremy Bentham concluded that a decision is democratic if it gives

---

[4] Unfortunately—'what can go wrong will go wrong' (Murphy's law)—the architects who later built the House of Commons chose an adversarial chamber of two sides, one facing the other, both of which could then hurl abuse at each other… which is what they did. The word 'tory' for example was slang for 'Irish papist bandit' (Churchill, 1956: Book II, 224).

the greatest good to the greatest number... the superlative of the superlative. Since then, many have made the mistake of trying to identify this ideal superlative in a voting procedure which is only comparative—the wretched binary vote—a process which defies logic and which, we now know, was and still is often guaranteed to fail.

One of the first to realise its inadequacies was Ramón Llull, in 1299—once described as 'one of the most inspired madmen who ever lived,' (*ibid*: 19). This Spanish Catalan is now no doubt gyrating in his grave: when Catalonia held its binary referendum in 2017, one of the worst albeit non-fatal instances of violence in Barcelona was outside the Ramón Llull University. What an irony! The present rulers praise their forebear... but ignore his teachings! That referendum was yet another binary nonsense in which manipulatory rulers decided that only one option was to be on the ballot paper, 'Independence, yes or no?' and the voting procedure of their decision-making was just like that of an election in North Korea.

6.3.1 Preferential Voting

The next philosopher to take up the baton of preferential voting was a Cardinal in the Catholic Church, Nicholas Cusanus. And while Llull was in favour of either the Borda or the Condorcet rule (as they came to be called), the Cardinal was very much an advocate of the former. "With much study," he wrote in 1433, "I have not been able to find a safer system, and believe me, no more perfect system can be found" (Sigmund, 1963: 212). He was (like the current author, not very modest perhaps... but) spot on.

So you might think that the good cardinals would adopt such a system for the election of a new pope. Might you? No no. The modified Borda count MBC cannot easily be controlled. Accordingly, as elsewhere in politics, the powers that be—not the divine ones now, just the (sometimes not very) humble human ones—prefer to retain total control... so they continued to use majority voting. No wonder the process of choosing a new pope sometimes took (and can still take) quite a long time: when there's no majority in favour of any one obvious cardinal candidate, (here we go again)... they resort to a whole string of majority votes; the process may take far longer than any *baraza*, *gacaca* or Mongolian assembly. Their record was set in 1268–1271 when the assembled cardinals—every one of them holy, no doubt, and old for sure—voted on umpteen candidates... but, yet again, there was a majority against every proposed candidate. Eventually, after sitting outside for weeks... months... years... the hopeful, mindful, prayerful faithful became playful: they took the roof off! This would make it easier, they reckoned, for the Holy Spirit to inspire the good cardinals… before yet another one died. Sure enough—whether the weather went wet is not known—the assembled quickly found their collective, or at least their majority will—well one of the majority wills. It had taken 33 months and three deaths!

6.4   The History of Social Choice Science

In 1948, when the Scot, Duncan Black, decided to write a book on voting theory, he didn't intend to write anything on its origins… because he "did not even know that it had a history" (Black, 1987: xi). As these pages relate, the science of social choice as it is now called nevertheless goes back a long way, and it has been reborn many times.

One of the most influential re-incarnations, some 300 years or more after Cusanus, was in France in the 1780s. Revolution was in the air. And manipulation was in the Assembly of the Notables. A certain Monsieur Calonne had the support of only 44 of the 140 members. Umm, problems. How can you control 140 when you have only 44 of them? Ah ha! Clever boy. He divided the 140 into 7 sub-committees, each of 20 members—all, so far, very fair. Four of these committees were a mixture, 11 of his own supporters, and 9 of the others—so he had a majority of 11:9 in these 4 committees; the other 3 consisted only of his opponents, so he had nothing, a 'minority' of 0 in all 3 of them. Now needless to say, democracy and all that, every dispute was reduced to a binary choice, so all seven committees took their decisions on their various disputes by majority vote. Umm, solutions. M Calonne won everything! He had an 11:9 majority on 4 committees; next, when all 7 committees met, he had a 4:3 majority. Perfect (Paine, 1985: 97).

Mathematically it reads:

$$44 \geq \frac{140}{2} + 1$$

which, of course, is nonsense.

L'Académie des Sciences was a little more scientific. Two if its members—Le Marquis de Condorcet and Chevalier Jean-Charles de Borda—invented (or reinvented) the two voting procedures which today bear their names. *L'Académie* had a debate about which one was better, and eventually chose the Borda Count BC as it came to be called (even though the Cusanus Count might have been the fairer title). It was used partly for decision-making but mainly as an electoral system, and it worked quite well.

Unfortunately, however, they changed the

$$(m, m - 1 \ldots 1) \qquad (\{\text{rule(i)}\})$$

which we first encountered in para 2.4, into

$$(n, n - 1 \ldots 1) \text{ or } (n - 1, n - 2 \ldots 0) \qquad (\{\text{rules(ii) and (iii)}\}.)$$

This meant that, with the m rule, the points awarded to a 1st preference depended on how many preferences the voter has cast; while with an n or $(n-1)$ formula, the points awarded depended on the number of options listed on the ballot. As we implied in that para 2.4, the m rule promotes consensus, the n rules incentivise intransigence.

So, inevitably, when voting, some of the members started to truncate their votes. No wonder M de Borda exclaimed, "My scheme is intended only for honest [voters]" (Black, 1987:182).

These were turbulent times, of course. 1789 witnessed the revolution and, shortly afterwards, Napoléon came to power. Needless to say, he of all people didn't like this 'consensus nonsense', (para 1.1), so *l'Académie* reverted to majority voting, and Napoléon had the first of his three binary referendums in 1800 for the world's first 'chilly democratic morn'. The science was dead, again. And many people today, in France, know little or nothing about M Jean-Charles de Borda.[5]

6.4.1 The Science Re-born

The next advocate of preferential points voting, in line with Llull and Cusanus, was another pious fellow, Rev. Charles Dodgson. He wrote a few pamphlets on voting and stuff, but he really should have written a book on the subject... alas (or not alas), he wrote *Alice* instead, *Alice in Wonderland*. Lewis Carroll.

All of which brings us up to the present day, to the now well-established Science of Social Choice, and all credit goes to Duncan Black (mentioned above) and Kenneth Arrow, (whom we met in para 5.2, Footnote 3). In the latter's impossibility theorem, he argued that nothing is perfect, that Condorcet is prone to the paradox (para 1.3.2) and that Borda might suffer

---

[5] In 2006, I was invited to go to France to address a French Green Party Conference in Coutances, Normandy, on decision-making. So it was that I spoke to a whole load of French people about a Frenchman they'd never heard of!

from an irrelevant alternative, (para 2.5). But he also said "… the method of majority decision satisfies [several] conditions when there are only two alternatives" (Arrow, 1963: 46). So maybe he wasn't perfect either: that last statement is almost meaningless, because in politics, as we said in para 2.1, there are almost never only two alternatives, or shouldn't be, or wouldn't be if the question were asked properly.

Alas, the science is still relatively unknown. The people who still need to be convinced, or even taught, are umpteen politicians, countless journalists, and numerous academics, many of whom argue at length about electoral systems but, as implied in the Preface, say little or nothing about binary vote decision-making. In brief, lots of decision-makers do not know how best to make decisions. Indeed, "… the theory of voting… appears to be wholly unknown to anyone concerned with its practical application. It is certainly quite unknown to the politicians… [and] to experts in political institutions…" (Dummett, 1984: 5). And here's another: "… there is a surprisingly strong and persistent tendency in political science to equate democracy solely with majoritarian democracy and to fail to recognise consensus democracy as an alternative and equally legitimate type."[6] (Lijphart, 2012: 6.)

6.4.2   The Lessons Unlearnt

Thus the world blunders from one majoritarian "cold morn" to another, and binary majority votes have often been the harbinger if not the instrument of death. In 1903, at a meeting of the Russian Social Democratic Workers' Party in London, the members took a vote on party membership. Lenin lost, 23–28. Ha, never mind comrades, he said, "I do not think our differences are so important" (Deutscher, 1982: 71). Some of those present got a bit fed up with all this arguing and walked out.[7] Lenin now had his chance. On the next vote, he won, 19–17, with 3 abstentions. Oh but this was important, apparently—the relatively minor detail of who should edit their magazine. So they split. He called his winning faction the Bolsheviks—the word means 'members of the majority' from the Russian word for 'majority', 'bolshinstvo' (большинство)—even though he didn't have a majority but only the largest minority: 19 of 39. And the others, the (other) minority, became the Mensheviks from 'menshinstvo' (меньшинство), 'minority'.

---

[6] Admittedly, Lijphart is talking of consociationalism, which as we know is still binary.

[7] They were, after all, in London. Not every comrade had the chance of such tourism. Maybe they went for a pint.

In 1933, Hitler won a weighted majority vote, the Enabling Act, not least by some underhand tactics like banning all the communists and promising segregated education to the Centre Party. Only the Socialists voted against, so in March, he got the required 2/3rds weighted majority. Next, in November, Hitler held the first of his four referendums, just to make it all 'democratic': 93% in favour on a 92% turnout.

In China, where villagers elect their village councils, (para 5.4, Footnote 12), Máo Zédōng was yet another majoritarian. It really is odd, to put it at its mildest, that the West should suggest that China should use majority vote decision-making, when it was the Chinese who (along with the Greeks) first used majority voting (para 6.2.3); when it was China which first used multi-option voting, (para 6.3), which many in the West have yet to even sample; when it was in China that majority voting was used in village tribunals as sentences of death; this was during the Great Leap Forward, 1958–62, the anti-Rightist campaign—one of the world's worst examples of binary politics; and when (it is said by some though disputed by others) the Chinese Communist Party Politburo Standing Committee used a majority vote in its 1989 decision to order military intervention into Tiān'ānmén Square, (Fenby, 2012: 180; Zhao, 2010: 29), perhaps by a margin of just one vote, (Emerson, 2020: 167).

Now to the Balkans. The Soviet Union collapsed in 1991, as too, like dominoes, the communist countries in eastern Europe—not least Yugoslavia, where the European Commission's "insistence on referendums... provided the impetus... to create ethnically pure areas through population transfers and expulsions," (Woodward, 1995: 271). A *binary* referendum, in Bosnia? How mad can you get? In the wake of a very divisive multi-party election (or sectarian head-count) in 1991, a two-round TRS contest, Bosnia which had been part of the secular state of Yugoslavia was now 40:30:20, Muslim:Orthodox:Catholic. So there was no majority anyway. As we mentioned in the Preface, the referendum was held... and it started the war.[8]

Next, Africa. Two years after the start of the Bosnia war, the *Interahamwe* initiated the 1994 genocide in Rwanda with the slogan quoted in the Preface, *"rubanda nyamwinshi,"* 'we are the majority," (Prunier, 1995: 183). But first, some more history: a century earlier, in 1892 at the Battle of Mengo, just

---

[8] In October 1991, six months before that fatal referendum, as was mentioned in the Acknowledgements, I invited a guest from Sarajevo to attend a cross-community conference in Belfast, to warn against any such binary ballot.

north of today's Rwanda/Uganda border, the *wafaranza* fought the *wain-gereza*,[9] and many were killed. The former had been converted to Christianity by French missionaries, so they were Catholics; the latter, by Scottish Presbyterians, were Protestants; and the war, a religious conflict, was fought in a continent which some Europeans called primitive... but a cause of that war was these imported European beliefs. Likewise, in 1994, the genocide was to a huge extent caused by western ideas (sometimes called ideals)—the belief in and practice of majority rule, (Emerson, 2012: 15–16).

The civil war in Yemen is yet another majority-versus-minority conflict, this one between the two sects of Islam, Sunni and Shi'a. Indeed, this rivalry is throughout the Middle East, and the problems of Palestine/Israel are also, of course, binary.

6.4.3   Referendums

And so it goes on. There is often dysfunctional politics in so-called 'stable democracies' like the United States, or Malaysia, or Britain, and despite the violent history of binary plebiscites in Northern Ireland in 1973, in the 1990s in the Balkans and the Caucasus (Emerson, 2012: 21), in Timor Leste in 1999, and, worst of all, in South Sudan in 2011,[10] there is still widespread talk of yet more binary referendums, all over the place:

- Kashmir (as per the UN Resolution of 1947); yet any such poll would (probably) be a bloodbath!
- Scotland, where the Scottish National Party SNP used to be in favour of a multi-option referendum... but now that the SNP itself is in power, now that they can control (manipulate) the question, they appear to have changed their minds. And all this, despite the fact that the word Scotland—*Shotlandiya*, Шотландия—was used by Russian separatists in eastern Ukraine, where referendums have already been held, in Crimea, Donetsk and Luhansk (para 7.2).[11] And just as Catalonia ignores its Ramón Llull, so too Scotland knows little of Duncan Black.

---

9 Swahili words meaning 'French-speaking' and 'English-speaking' respectively.

10 In a 2011 unAfrican (Chap. 2, Footnote 1) referendum, 98.8% voted in favour of independence, a form of power-sharing quickly collapsed, and South Sudan imploded.

11 Referendums were held in all four places in 2014; Scotland's was legal, the others not. Such 'minor' details, of course, were not debated in Luhansk. (In this year of 2014, I was an election observer for the OSCE in Ukraine—my tenth deployment over there—and also in Scotland, for my second in Edinburgh.).

- Catalonia... despite the fact that one place which is watching intently to see if an illegal referendum can be held successfully is Republika Srpska, which is also rattling both its sabres and its ballot boxes.
- Northern Ireland. According to the Belfast Agreement, (para 1.4.1), there may well be a referendum on the constitutional status... sometime. Umpteen academics from University College London and elsewhere recently reviewed all the possible ramifications of all the possible courses of action... except one: the suggestion of taking a preliminary non-binding multi-option poll, which their reports did not even list, let alone mention, let alone discuss. The *idée* is indeed *fixe*, as in concrete.
- Hong Kong, Taiwan, Xīnjiāng and Tibet, in any of which binary politics could be at least dangerous.

6.5 Conclusion

The history of the world shows that many people have questioned that which seems to be an archetypal form of behaviour—the tendency to reduce every political dispute to a binary conflict of two mutually opposed options. Those who pursue a binary approach do so because they regard the dispute as a win-or-lose contest which they want to win... and in which their chances of winning would be much reduced if the dispute were not binary.

Sadly, at the cost of countless lives, political leaders do not want to change this *modus operandi*. What I find quite extraordinary, however, is the fact that many commentators—journalists and academics and writers *et al*— still think majority voting is not only OK, but that to use any other decision-making methodology might not be OK.

Democracy, they say, is majority rule... which (I repeat) is true. And a democratic majority opinion, they continue, can be identified in a majority vote. Which is nonsense. The trouble comes in their next line of binary thinking: he who criticises the democratic practice of majority voting is not pro-democracy and must therefore be anti-democracy, anti-democratic. At best misguided, at worst...

But let us learn the lessons of history and let us dream. What would the world be like if at all levels of government, decisions were taken in consensus, either in a verbal consensus or by using a consensus vote? What could the world be like if politicians used voting procedures in which their ambitions could best be realised if they did not compete, but cooperated? Wow! What a lovely dream! And it could all come true. It's in Chap. 7.

References

Arrow, K. J. (1963). *Social choice and individual values*, Yale University Press, New Haven and London.

Black, D. (1987). *The theory of committees and elections*, Kluwer Academic Publishers, Massachusetts.

Churchill, W. (1956). *A history of the english-speaking peoples*, Cassell, London.

Dahl, R. A. (1998). *On democracy*, Yale University Press, New Haven and London.

De Ste Croix, G. E. M. (2005). *Athenian democratic origins*, Oxford University Press, Oxford.

Deutscher, I. (1982). *Stalin*, Penguin, Hammondsworth, England.

Dummett, M. (1984). *Voting procedures*, Oxford University Press, Oxford.

Emerson, P. (2012). *Defining democracy*, 2nd edition, Springer, Heidelberg.

Emerson, P. (2020). *Majority voting as a catalyst of populism*, Springer, Heidelberg.

Fenby, J. (2012). *Tiger head snake tails*, Simon and Shuster, London.

Franke, H., & Twitchett, D. (1994). *Cambridge history of China*, Vol. 6, Cambridge University Press, Cambridge.

Kapuściński, R. (2001). *The shadow of the sun*, Penguin, London.

Lijphart, A. (2012). *Patterns of democracy*, 2nd Edition, Yale University Press, New Haven and London.

McLean, I., & Urken, A. B. (1995). *Classics of social choice*, Ann Arbor, The University of Michigan Press, Michigan.

Mandela, N. (1994). *Long walk to freedom*, Abacus, London.

Mote, F. W. (2015). *Imperial China, 900–1800*. Harvard University Press, Cambridge, Massachusetts.

Paine, T. (1985). *The rights of man*, Part II, Penguin, London.

Prunier, G. (1995). *The Rwanda crisis*, C Hurst and Co., London.

Sen, A. (2021). *Home in the world*, Allen Lane, Dublin.

Sigmund, P. E. (1963). *Nicholas of cusa and medieval thought*, Harvard University Press, Cambridge, Massachusetts.

Sigmund, P. E. (1966). *The ideologies of the developing nations*, Frederick A Praeger, New York.

Wang, Y.-C. (1968). an outline of the central government of the former han dynasty. In J. L. Bishop (Ed.), *Studies of Government Institutions in Chinese History*. Harvard-Yenching Institute Studies XXIII. Harvard University Press, Cambridge, Massachusetts.

Which, (2017). *Socialist Constitution of the Democratic People's Republic of Korea*. Foreign Languages Publishing House, Pyongyang.

Woodward, S. (1995). *Balkan tragedy*, The Brookins Institution, Washington.

Zhao, Z. (2010). *Prisoner of the state*, Pocket Books, London.

7

A Consensual Milieu

… by not publicizing what can go wrong, by not informing the general public how to avoid these problems [of bad decision-making], expect to experience societal consequences that are significant and serious.

Donald Saari, *Disposing Dictators, Demystifying Voting Paradoxes*, p. 217.

Abstract The term 'democratic leader' is perhaps an oxymoron, and maybe no less so than the slogan some of these elected 'leaders' often criticise: 'democratic centralism.' Basically, politics is often flooded with critics criticising their critics. But the aggressive comments with which many politicians attack their opponents have a profound impact on society, especially on the young. Those in power perform in this way, partly because of the adversarial structure of politics. The need, therefore, for a democratic polity which is non-adversarial—in a word, for voting procedures which are inherently 'peaceful'—cannot be over-emphasised. The benefits could be huge.

Keywords Consensus · Win–win politics · Conflict resolution · Conflict prevention · Evolution · Climate change

7.1 Introduction

Imagine, if politicians weren't arguing the whole time, if instead they were co-operating with each other—as do other persons in other positions of authority in society—what a superb example that would be for the young, not

© The Author(s), under exclusive license to Springer Nature
Switzerland AG 2022
P. Emerson, *The Punters' Guide to Democracy*,
https://doi.org/10.1007/978-3-031-06987-1_7

least for the teenagers of inner-city gangs in deprived areas and/or sectarian ghettoes. After all, many political disputes are multi-option discussions which have degenerated into binary arguments; and racism, sectarianism and xenophobia often start with a binary mindset: 'us' and 'them', 'us' versus 'the others'.

Executive committees of community groups, management boards of companies, trades unions executives, university administrations… these folks often manage to work together pretty well (though they too have their moments). In fact, some organisations never use majority votes in decision-making, and deliberately so; instead, they rely on a purely verbal approach, while a few resort to a more inclusive form of voting, sometimes approval voting, and occasionally the modified Borda count MBC.[1] There is no earthly reason why elected representatives couldn't do the same; it would help enormously because, as we saw in Chap. 4, the introduction of a non-adversarial voting procedure could change their divisive structure of governance.

In effect, a most immediate benefit of moving from the adversarial binary vote to the more accurate and therefore more democratic preferential ballot could be the more civilised behaviour of our elected politicians. Their example could help all those trying to promote a more tolerant society, to improve race relations, and so on.

There are a few other benefits too, which we'll now try to list. From one country to the next, preferential decision-making could:

- in conflict zones, help not just the process of resolution and reconciliation, but also the more permanent goal of violence prevention;
- on the international scene, be a key to ensuring the current rivalry between (increasingly authoritarian) democracies and (partially democratic) one-party states remains non-violent;
- not only in the USA and Europe, make more difficult any further acquisitions of power by right-wing extremists, or by other, sometimes violent extremists of the left, or by fanatics of a religious bent;
- everywhere and forever, cater more peacefully for the future evolution of our species;
- everywhere, enable every nation to tackle more effectively the problems of Covid and Climate Change.

Phew. That's quite a few. Let's take them one at a time.

---

[1] One interesting example of a Borda points system was in the first use of participatory budgeting in Porte Allegre in Brazil in 1989; another was in Ireland in the 2016 Citizens' Assembly (even though the official report 'pretended' that their decision-making was all majoritarian—maybe because of majority-vote stipulations in its terms of reference).

7.2   Conflict Resolution

If a people want to live in a great big place, and if a majority of them so decide, then of course, they may. That's democracy, they say. If however a minority of that majority want to opt out, and if a majority of that minority vote to opt out, then of course they may. That's democracy, they say again. But if a majority of a minority of that minority of that majority vote to opt out of opting out and to opt back in again, then they may do that as well. That too is democracy, they still say. Yet again, binary voting is a nonsense, and a dangerous nonsense.

When Ireland opted out of the UK in 1920, Northern Ireland opted out of Ireland and back into the UK. Hence the Troubles as they were called, 1969–1994/8.

When Croatia and then Bosnia opted out of Yugoslavia, the Krajina[2] tried to opt out of Croatia, and Republika Srpska tried to opt out of Bosnia. Both countries erupted into war. In another part of the whole, Kosovo[3] also held a referendum on independence in 1991, but this result—99% in favour on an 87% turnout—was not internationally recognised until after the 1999 war.

When Armenia, Azerbaijan and Georgia opted out of the old Soviet Union in 1991, Nagorno-Karabakh opted out of Azerbaijan and tried, unsuccessfully, to opt in to Armenia—the dispute rumbles on, and in 2020 it was war, again; back in the early 1990s, Abkhazia and South Ossetia opted out of Georgia, for two more wars... or series of wars. "*Matrioshka*[4] nationalism," the Russians called it, (Reid, 2003: 136), or they used to before they themselves started fighting the Georgians in 2008 and the Ukrainians in 2014.

And in Ukraine, in 1991, every region (*oblast*) voted in a national referendum on independence, and every region, including Crimea, Donetsk and Luhansk, voted in favour. In 2014, however, each of these three had another referendum and, supposedly, changed their minds. In total effect: Ukraine opts out of the USSR—the big out of the enormous; next, Donetsk opts out of Ukraine—the small out of the big; and then parts of the Donetsk *oblast*[5] tried to opt out of opting out (of Ukraine) and to opt back in again—the

---

[2] The Krajina were three mainly Orthodox (Serb) parts of mainly Catholic Croatia.

[3] The Serbs write Kosovo, or even Kosovo and Metohija, while Albanians prefer Kosova... but both are right.

[4] The famous Russian dolls, inside one of which there is a smaller one, and then a tiny one, and then a miniscule one....

[5] The regions of Dobropillia and Krasnoarmiisk, plus seven village councils, nearly three million people in all participated, and by a majority of 69.1%, they voted for 'Peace, order and the unity of Ukraine'.

tiny out of the small. Three more *matrioshki*. The law is an ass, in Ireland, the former Yugoslavia, the Caucasus, Ukraine, everywhere, it is an ass.

So one way of helping to avoid conflict would be to re-define the right of self-determination. It was first coined by President Wilson in 1916 to help resolve the *external* problem of colonisation; it was never intended to address *internal* problems of secession. Most importantly, the instrument of secession should not be a blunt binary ballot: it should not be possible for a whole people to be determined by only a (50% + 1 type) majority of them.

7.2.1 Binary Voting in Binary Conflicts

Here's another anomaly: whenever diplomats and others meet to discuss peace settlements, they invariably talk about electoral systems and, as often as not, come down in favour of proportional representation PR. The one exception of note refers to the electoral system chosen for Lebanon where, as we saw in para 5.2.2, the indigenous folk devised a very 'peaceful' form of first-past-the-post FPTP. Generally speaking, however, most peace negotiators manage to come up with a pretty good electoral system.

But, it seems, they all get stuck on binary voting. It is indeed an *idée fixe*. Most politicians don't consider preferential decision-making voting systems, (para 6.4.1), and nor do most diplomats. In some scenarios, in the knowledge that binary voting—simple or weighted majority voting—is problematic, they might tweak it a little. Sometimes, for example, they adopt the idea of double voting: accordingly, if a law is to be passed, it must have the support, in Belgium, of both the Flemings and the Walloons; in Northern Ireland, of both the Protestants and the Catholics; in Cyprus, of both the Greek- and the Turkish-Cypriots; and so on. In English, we use the word 'consociational', which is a bit of a mouthful; the Belgians call it special voting. Unfortunately, these negotiators seldom go any further; they don't look at multi-option and preferential procedures.

Instead, they get stuck; and part of the subsequent trouble of this sort of consociational decision-making is, of course, the veto: just 51% of any group can veto everything, even if it's supported by 99% of all the others. Now a veto has been described as being similar to a pistol in a Chekhov play: if it's there on the mantelpiece in Act I, then, sure enough, it will be used in Act II.

It's bad enough in a two-part society like the ones we've just mentioned. But in Bosnia where there are three? This power-sharing feature was insti-gated in Bosnia, before the 1992–5 war, after the first multi-party elections in 1990; so all three religious groupings[6] had the veto; "In its eighteen-month-long existence, the Bosnian parliament failed to pass a single law," (Glenny, 1992: 148).

7.2.2   Binary Voting in Stable Democracies

This crazy notion—that electoral systems can be good but decision-making must be binary—applies not only to peace settlements. In 1949, when Germany's Parliamentary Council met in Bonn, sure enough, they looked at the electoral system, and for some reason, they blamed the failings of Weimar on the pre-war electoral system of PR-list, and hence today's multi-member proportional MMP (para 5.2.11). But they did not apportion blame to Weimar's binary decision-making. The latter, apparently, was/is just fine. Indeed, in the Introduction to the *Grundgesetz*, the current *Basic Law*, they write: "The fact that Members of the *Bundestag* (parliament) take decisions on behalf of the whole German people... is a requirement... for majority decision-making. In most cases... a simple majority of votes cast" (*Op. cit.* 1998: 18.). This is pure gobbledegook.

Mathematically it's even worse than what we had in para 6.4. In its most extreme case, it means:

$$a = (50\% + 1) \times a$$

which, of course, is just more nonsense.

The founding fathers in the USA were similarly obsessed with binary decision-making. Many of them were totally opposed to the two-party system of politics: "The alternate domination of one faction over another," said George Washington in his farewell address in Gettysburg in 1796, "has perpetrated the most horrid enormities [and] is itself a frightful despotism." But neither he nor his colleagues identified the cause of this binary despotism to be binary voting. On electoral systems, they were sometimes quite insightful: Thomas Jefferson for example, actually invented a form of PR. On decision-making, however, no. Yet again, for many, that just has to be binary. So the USA adopted a divisive polity, and the USA is now divided. Donald Trump was/is only the denouement of a binary polity.

---

[6] There are no ethnic differences in Bosnia, apart from those of the smaller minorities like the Vlah and the Roma. The three big groupings—the Bosniaks, Croats and Serbs—are all Slavs, Yugo (i.e. southern) Slavs; Muslim, Catholic and Orthodox Slavs.

If only, oh if only, peace negotiations would recommend, not just 'peaceful' electoral systems—the best of which we now know are the more inclusive and therefore preferential forms of PR—but also 'peaceful' decision-making.

In QBS, (para 5.2.12), the voter who so wishes may treat an election as his/her individual act of reconciliation: he can vote for his favourite, one of 'his own' candidates perhaps, but he can also vote for a compromise candidate or two, including perhaps those from the other ethno-religious grouping(s), those who during the conflict had actually been the enemy.

In decision-making, it should be the same: for those who wish, a vote could be 'peaceful'—a full ballot stating, not only their 1st preference, but also their compromise option(s). This can happen if the procedure itself is preferential. Furthermore, such an inclusive decision-making methodology might also help to ensure that the relevant peace settlement survives the test of time. A decision on any one policy shall be taken if there is at least a minimum threshold level of consensus support for that decision. If not—to take a Ukrainian example, if there is no consensus in 2014 to seek membership of NATO—then no decision shall be taken.

7.2.3   Conflict Prevention

If all-party power-sharing were the international, democratic norm, a major cause of conflict would be no more, not least in Israel/Palestine where the current (binary) interpretation of majority rule makes the ideal, a single-state solution, impossible.

The same applies to Russia which tries to justify its incursions into Ukraine on the basis that some Ukrainians are 'ethnic Russians', even though there is no such ethnicity. The Ukrainians are nearly all Slavs—just like their cousins, the Yugoslavs (para 7.2.1, Footnote 5)—except for a few minorities like the Crimean Tatars. At the same time, there are lots of Russians in Russia who are not Slav at all: in Europe, there are the Udmurts and the Maris, for example, all living to the west of the Urals; in the Northern Caucasus, there are the Ingushetians, the Chechens and others, all again non-Slav; while on the eastern side of those Ural mountains, in Siberia, there's everything from the Buryats near Lake Baikal to the Chukchis on the shores of the Bering Sea, non-Slavs, the lot of them!

China is another complex problem. Some say the Uighurs should have their own state. In which case, where? After all, the latter originally came from somewhere in Mongolia where in the 8th Century, during the Táng Dynasty, they fought not *against* but *with* the Chinese against the Eastern Turk Khaganate. And if the Uighurs are to be given home-rule, somewhere, then what about some of the other peoples, the Tangut and the Xiōngnú, we mentioned, let alone the other 50-odd minorities already recognised in China.

In brief, not every ethnicity or tribe should have its own nation-state, lest there be a hundred odd nations in what is now the Russian Federation, quite a few more in China, and literally thousands in Africa. Furthermore, the establishment of a jurisdiction on a religious criterion—the partition of Ireland in 1920, Protestant and Catholic; of the Indian sub-continent in 1947, Muslim and Hindu; of Palestine in 1947, Arab and Jew; of Yugoslavia in the 1990s, Catholic, Muslim and Orthodox; of Timor in 2002, Catholic and Muslim—should not be repeated.

So maybe the concept of nation-state has had its day. Let us nevertheless accept that which we have inherited, as much by historical accident rather than by any divine, natural or geographical providence, and let's aim for the democratisation of everywhere. We have our national identities, that's for sure; but we also have our regional and local identities, as well as our common human identity. And we must learn to live 'with' each other; well we can't best do that if we are forever making decisions ('for' or) 'against' each other, declaring ourselves to be 'this' or 'that' while denying that, well, maybe, we're a bit of both if not a mixture of more, and perhaps much else besides.

7.3   The West, Russia and China

In Washington, Congress takes decisions by majority vote, sometimes by the tiny margin of only one vote.[7] In Beijing, the Congress uses the same methodology. One of Dèng Xiǎopíng's first reforms was to "replace a single-leader dominant system, based on a cult of personality, with a collective leadership that made decisions in a consensual fashion (even voting when necessary)"[8] (Shambaugh, 2021: 118.). Admittedly, some of the votes taken in Beijing involve overwhelming margins, (as in Northern Ireland's 1973 Border Poll which won a 98.9% 'yes' from a 58.7% turnout—para 1.4.1). In March 2013 for example, Xí Jìnpíng, was confirmed in office in the 12th National People's Congress by a majority of 2,952 to 1 against, with 3 abstentions; in contrast, in the Congress of 1992, "about one third of all delegates… voted against or abstained in a vote to support the central leadership's

---

[7] For an overview of just some of the many votes around the world where the margin of victory or defeat has sometimes been a singleton—sometimes the ballot of a deputy who has been bribed, threatened or seduced—see *Won by One* on http://www.deborda.org/won-by-one/.

[8] A bit of a contradiction, I would argue, but the sense is clear.

proposed Three Gorges Dam project," (Wright, 2019: 30). Nevertheless, the procedure in both congresses—American and Chinese—is the same: a binary vote.

In a chamber of 435 (in the US House of Representatives) or 2,980 (in China's 13th National People's Congress of 2017/18), taking a binary vote where there are just two ways of voting can all be transparent and open—though whether the choice of options in either venue was taken so openly may not be the case. Those present just raise a hand in favour of one or other option, and someone with an abacus does the count.

7.3.1 Choice

You cannot, however, take a multi-option preferential vote by a show of hands quite so easily. With three options in a plurality vote, there are those three ways of voting—**A, B** or **C**—which makes life difficult. But in preference voting, there are the six possible ways of filling in the ballot—**A-B-C, A-C-B, B-A-C, B-C-A, C-A-B** and **C-B-A**, (as we said in para 2.3.1)—which means it's next to impossible. We went on to say that with four or five options, up to 24 or 120 different opinions or nuances may be expressed, every opinion a set of preferences, every set a reading on the calibrated instrument. Preferential voting is indeed a precision tool, perfectly capable of catering for the diversity of our species, but definitely not suitable for 'a show of hands'.

With a smartphone, however, members can just click—3-2-5-1-4, whatever—wait for a nanosecond or few, and then view the voters' profile. In other words, the introduction of computers into the debating chambers of the world, and the use of these multi-option technologies in their decision-making, could mean that the structures of governance between today's competing 'ideologies' could begin to merge even more.

7.4   Right, Extreme Right and Downright Wrong

For many people, the ideal of an all-party power-sharing executive gives cause to pause. After all, there are those who would not want to sit in the same cabinet with others of extreme views, violent 'left-wing' or 'right-'… fanatical 'Christian' or 'Islamic'… whatever, (para 4.4.1). At the same time, the extremists themselves might not be too keen on all this 'consensus nonsense'.

Now it is generally accepted that women are more likely to be elected with PR, (IDEA, 1997: 30). In a nutshell, the better the electoral system, the fairer the result. Likewise in decision-making: if the question is binary, the outcome could all too easily be an extremist policy. Hence, by the same coin, the better the decision-making methodology, the better the decision.

In 2016, Trump would almost certainly not have been elected president, if the USA had had a fair electoral system; nor would he have been able to get some of his policies through Congress if the latter based its decision-making on a fair and preferential process. Likewise, also in 2016, the UK would probably not have voted for Brexit, if the ballot paper had offered a range of, say, 4–5 options, (para 1.2, Footnote 3).

Professor Iain McLean once described it like this: if your bike goes wrong, you fall off, and you are immediately aware that something is wrong. When a voting system goes wrong, however, most are totally oblivious of anything amiss.

The subject is just so important. In many European countries, if consensus voting were to be introduced, now, today, it might be possible to avoid the acquisition of power by the extreme right. If, however, we do not change our decision-making, and if such a party does gain 50% + 1, it will be too late. The horse will have bolted. In the USA, the situation is perhaps even more desperate: their political structure should be changed now, immediately, lest Trump or another Trumpian runs for the White House in 2024.

In summary, if the world is to avoid the emergence of extremist leaders into elected positions of authority—the likes of Vladimir Putin—it should adopt not only a good electoral system plus accurate and inclusive decision-making, but also an inclusive structure of governance, with preferential voting in its parliaments. As an absolute minimum, the world should not be led by singletons: every democracy should have all-party (and/or all-inclusive) power-sharing, and anything else is not very democratic.

7.4.1 Interference

With today's computers and so on, hacking into another country's election is all too easy; this is certainly true if the victim uses a simple and simplistic FPTP electoral system, and especially true if its political structure is that of a two-party state. {And let's remember these words, first written in 1863: "The influence of Russia is expressed only in an unfavourable light: by intimidation at elections…" (Tolstoy, 2016: 22).} If, however, whatever malpractice is being hatched involves persuading people to change not just one but six preferences, such interference becomes much more difficult.

7.5   Evolution

Binary decision-making caters for the politics of the pendulum. In comes Obamacare. Next, after an election, it's out. Then, another election, and it's in again. A Martian would know this 'short-term-ism' is madness, let alone a member of the Chinese Communist Party, let alone everybody.

In consensus politics, such collective oscillations and vacillations are much reduced. Imagine, from one election to the next, increasing awareness of Climate Change, for example, sees a 2% swing in public opinion in favour of environmentalism. In which case, come the next general election, there should be a 2% swing, roughly, amongst those elected to parliament, and also, roughly, to the all-party power-sharing executive.

Or take another, much older topic. In centuries long gone, arranged marriages were often the norm. Gradually, over the years, many societies adopted a more liberal approach. The historian is able to pin-point the changing nature of a nation's consensus… but not the politician, not if he is relying on binary voting. The latter's analysis will zig-zag from one side of the changing consensus to another, only ever approximating to the historical truth. So consensus politics could cater for the more natural—and more peaceful, non-Hegelian—evolution of our species.

Furthermore, win-or-lose elections are often won by pre-election budgets of tax cuts and other 'bribes', short-term policies which often put the environment and the longer term at risk. In effect, adversarial politics is bad for the planet. In contrast, win—win elections combined with post-election all-party power-sharing more readily focus on the long-term, which brings us to…

7.6   COVID, Climate Change and…

Follow the science, say the epidemiologists, especially in regard to Covid. Follow the science, say the environmentalists, in respect of Climate Change. Ignore the science, imply the decision-makers, (para 6.4.1).

With amazing speed, Covid is telling everybody that we humans must cooperate… or die. The same is true with Climate Change. We must all work together, and make decisions together, and follow through on their implementation together. Admittedly, sometimes, we try. At the 2021 Cop26 meeting in Scotland, those concerned in effect accepted that binary voting would be inappropriate. But nobody, it seems, thought of preference voting. Instead, it was back to the veto {and Chekhov—(para 7.2.1)}. Right at the end of the conference, the argument was binary: was conference going to 'phase down' or 'phase out' coal? India and China grabbed the veto from the mantelpiece and fired—bang!—the consensus was dead.

Cop27 should use consensus voting, as too should all international decision-making gatherings.

7.7 Conclusion

Homo sapiens might survive if it accepts that the collective good supersedes that of the individual. A billionaire does not have the right to zoom off into space, not, that is, if such a pursuit consumes more than his fair share of the world's finite resources. In like manner, countries like China, India and the US do not have the right to unlimited pollution. The individual human does not have unlimited rights, and the individual nation does not have unlimited sovereignty.

We have to take collective decisions, just as did our forebears everywhere. Today, however, we have the advantage that we can supplement their ancient wisdoms with our modern technologies: at last, the ideas of 800 years ago in China and 700 years ago in Europe can be combined with African (if not universal, archetypal) traditions and modern technology: we can facilitate our decision-making with preferential points voting. Thus may we be able to ensure, not just our immediate survival, but also our further peaceful evolution to a truly civilised, peaceful, democratic and sustainable future.

References

Aristotle. (1992). *The Politics*, Penguin, London.
German Federal Government. (1998). *Basic Law*, Press and Information Office, Bonn.
Glenny, M. (1992). *The Fall of Yugoslavia Penguin*, London.
IDEA Assistance. (1997). *Electoral System Design*, Institute for Democracy and Electoral IDEA, Stockholm.
Reid, A. (2003). *The Shaman's Coat*, Phoenix, London.
Saari, D. (2008). *Disposing Dictators, Demystifying Voting Paradoxes*, Cambridge University Press, Cambridge.
Shambaugh, D. (2021). *China's Leaders, from Mao to Now*, Polity, Cambridge.
Tolstoy, L. (2016). *The Cossacks*, Penguin, London.
Wright, T. (2019). *Party and State in post-Mao China*, Polity, London.

Epilogue: A Consensual Polity for a Consensual Milieu

"Simple majority decisions… cannot be fair in a democratic sense because the imposition of binary alternatives is itself unfair."

William H. Riker.

Liberalism against Populism, 1988, p 64.

Abstract Having criticised binary decision-making and its consequences, it is now time to define the more accurate methodology. Democratic decision-making is an inclusive process by which all concerned and/or their representatives may participate, both in formulating the options on which a decision is to be taken, and in then choosing the option which best represents the wishes of all. In other words, democracy should be inclusive and not adversarial, win–win and not win-or-lose. Decision-making with preferential points voting can cater for just such a political structure.

Keywords Democratic decision-making · Consensus · Collective will · Collective responsibility

The Principles

Democracy is for everybody. The people are superior to their parliament; their legislature is superior to the executive.

© The Editor(s) (if applicable) and The Author(s), under exclusive license to Springer Nature Switzerland AG 2022
P. Emerson, *The Punters' Guide to Democracy,*
https://doi.org/10.1007/978-3-031-06987-1

The separation of powers suggests that, as a general rule—i.e. for all non-urgent business—the executive does not propose legislation. (The legislature legislates; the executive 'only' executes).

In a *pluralist* democracy, controversies (if posed correctly) will be multi-optional.

A democratic decision is that which best represents the interests of all—the common good.

In debate, all relevant proposals which do not infringe the UN Charter shall be allowed 'on the table'.

In any vote, those involved—the people or their representatives—may cast their preferences freely. There shall be no whipped votes.

The Practice

A point of concern may be raised by any citizen, who may then contact an elected representative, whereupon the issue may be raised in the elected chamber. Other methodologies include the petition and a citizens' initiative.

When a problem does arise, parliament may decide to debate the issue, or to delegate the matter to a citizens' assembly or public enquiry. In (nearly) all such instances, the body concerned shall be tasked to take its decisions in consensus, either verbally and/or with a multi-option preferential vote.

Democratic decisions may be taken,

- either by the people themselves in referendums (a direct democracy);
- or in the elected chamber (a representative democracy) where the debate takes place in parliament;
- or in a mixture of the two.

No matter which way, controversial matters shall invariably be subject to a multi-option preferential ballot.

When a matter is raised and a possible option—the motion—is proposed, other parties may suggest alternatives; in a nutshell, every criticism should be positive, i.e. accompanied by an alternative proposal. Every party shall be entitled to one proposal. Amendments shall not be considered in the traditional binary way; rather, every suggestion shall be submitted as part of a complete package, and the debate shall centre on a choice of a few alternative motions, ideally all set out in a similar format.

Accordingly, in debate, all the various options shall be considered, and each may be amended, composited or even deleted, but only if the original

Table E.1 The debate

The Options	Parties' and their preferences				
	V	W	X	Y	Z
FPTP, first-past-the-post	1	-	-	3	5
PR-list open	2	4	1	2	3
FPTP + PR = MMP, multi-member proportional	3	3	2	1	4
PR-STV, single transferable vote	4	2	-	4	1
QBS, quota Borda system	5	1	-	5	2

proposer(s) agree to such a change. All contributions to the debate shall be limited both in time and/or word-length... and in total. There shall be no filibusters.

During the debate, the Speaker shall maintain a list of all options currently 'on the table', and parties may also 'lay their cards on the table', each declaring and adjusting their preferences on these various options, as the debate proceeds. To take a simple example, in a five-party parliament with parties V, W, X, Y and Z, in a debate on electoral systems, the various parties (having read Chap. 5) may each propose an option, their 1st preference, and also declare their 2nd and subsequent preferences on the other options.

The Speaker may display all this data, as shown in Table E.1: the options 'on the table' are listed in the left-hand column, and the parties' various preferences, thus far, in the shaded columns, alongside.

Each party has its 1st preference, but in stating their 2nd and subsequent preferences as well, all concerned can see where a consensus might lie. They say, in a majoritarian debate, "Once your fall-back positions are published, you have already fallen back to them" (Eban 1998: 81.) So all too often, those involved keep their cards close to their chest, revealing little, and negotiations can take an age. Consensus politics is more transparent.

If the matter is to be put to a vote, the Speaker shall draw up a balanced (short) list, usually of about 4–6 options, to represent the debate. If all concerned accept this list, they may proceed to cast their preferences.

A democratic decision shall be declared only if the winning option or composite surpasses a predetermined level of consensus support.

On highly contentious matters, the Speaker may stipulate that the final decision may be subject to a combined modified Borda count MBC/Condorcet count, whereupon the decision shall be taken as binding, only if the MBC winner is the same as the Condorcet social choice.

The Personnel

Participants in a citizens' assembly may be selected by lot, whereas in a public enquiry, they may be self-selected. The impartial non-voting commissioners in such bodies may be appointed or elected by parliament. Members of parliaments and regional/local councils shall all be elected, ideally in a preferential and proportional methodology, PR-STV or, better still, QBS, either in six-seater constituencies or in four- to six-seaters with a regional or national top-up.

Parliament's Speaker(s), always non-voting, may be appointed from outside any party structures, or elected from within those structures. In all such selections, at least two persons shall be appointed: the Speaker and a Deputy.

The executives of the elected chambers may be elected indirectly by those bodies, again in a preferential and proportional methodology, ideally a QBS matrix vote; or they may be elected directly by the people in a separate contest—as in a presidential election, in a simpler though still preferential ballot. Again, in this last instance, the election should always be for at least two persons—a president and a vice-president,[1] for example.

Very senior positions—that of president or prime minister—shall be subject to a time limit of so many terms or years. The same may also apply to ministerial appointments. In plural societies, ministerial posts may also be shared and/or rotated.

Conclusion

As democratic elected representatives, both in the legislature and in the executive, all such persons shall accept collective responsibility for the implementation of all democratic decisions taken, either in the elected chamber and/or in a referendum. Those who no longer wish to be democratic may resign.

References

Eban, A. (1998). *Diplomacy for the Next Century*. Yale University Press.

Riker, W. H. (1988). *Liberalism against Populism*. Waveland Press Inc.

---

[1] Such was the case originally in the US: US Constitution of 1787: Art II, para 1, Chap. 3.

Annex I: The Professors' Synopsis

I.1 Manifold Manipulation

Consider a committee of a dozen members. And imagine, they all agree that they don't like the status quo, option S. But they can't agree on its replacement: 5 want A, 4 want B and 3 want C. So majorities of 7, 8 and 9 don't want A, B and C respectively, and all of them, a majority of 12, don't want S. So there's a majority against everything. Being good democrats, however, they nevertheless take a vote. Let's assume the 12 have the preferences as shown. When one group moves a motion, the others propose amendments; next, they debate, (in this example, no-one changes their mind—that's politics); and finally, they vote (Table I.1).

If A is the motion, while B and C are the amendments, the debate is…

$$\{(B \text{ v } C) \text{ v } A\} \text{ v } S = \ldots$$

Table I.1 The Dozen's dilemma

Preferences	Numbers of voters and their preferences		
	5	4	3
1st	A	B	C
2nd	B	C	S
3rd	C	S	A
4th	S	A	B

© The Editor(s) (if applicable) and The Author(s), under exclusive
license to Springer Nature Switzerland AG 2022
P. Emerson, *The Punters' Guide to Democracy*,
https://doi.org/10.1007/978-3-031-06987-1

whereupon B beats C by 9:3; A beats B by 8:4; and S beats A by 7:5. So:

$$\{(B \vee C) \vee A\} \vee S = S.$$

However, if B is the motion, while A and C are the amendments, the debate is...

$$\{(A \vee C) \vee B\} \vee S = ...$$

whereupon C beats A by 7:5; B beats C by 9:3; and B beats S also by 9:3. So:

$$\{(A \vee C) \vee B\} \vee S = B.$$

And if C is the motion, while A and B are the amendments, the debate is...

$$\{(A \vee B) \vee C\} \vee S = ...$$

whereupon A beats B by 8:4; C beats A by 7:5; and C beats S by 12:0. So:

$$\{(A \vee B) \vee C\} \vee S = C.$$

Furthermore, if A is the status quo, while B, C and S take it in turns to be the motion and the two amendments, the outcome will be A. So if B is the motion, while C and S are the amendments, the debate is...

$$\{(C \vee S) \vee B\} \vee A = ...$$

whereupon C beats S by 12:0; B beats C by 9:3; and A beats B by 8:4. So:

$$\{(C \vee S) \vee B\} \vee A = A.$$

In like manner,

$$\{(B \vee S) \vee C\} \vee A = A$$

and

$$\{(B \vee C) \vee S\} \vee A = A$$

as well.

In all, in a multi-option debate, when there's no majority for any one option, the outcome of a *democratic* process based on binary voting can be anything: S (the status quo), or A or B or C! If on the other hand there is a majority for something the chair doesn't want, he can just add other options to split that majority, and still get the 'democratic' outcome he wants.

In other words, binary debates are manipulable... some politicians are manipulative... and many votes are indeed manipulated. It need not be so.

I.2 Conclusion

The above is a professors' synopsis of everyone else's Chapter 1. In brief, our current democratic decision-making is hopelessly unscientific, because it is (nearly always) binary... and this dualism can cause duels. Now one of the reasons why this majority voting is used, everywhere, is because so many professionals don't question its use. Hence this book. Hopefully, the professors and the press, and not only the punters, will read more than just this synopsis.

Annex II: More Manipulation

II.1 A Binary Lottery

In the voters' profile of Table 1.2, here repeated as Table II.1, when option **A**, artichokes, is the motion, while **B** and **C**, broccoli and cabbage, are the amendments, and option **D**, dill, is the (sort of) status quo, the outcome is option **D**, dill, as per Chap. 1's, Fig. 1.1b, here shown as Fig. II.1.

But what happens if the chef's *status quo* is option **A**? Again, we have a few possibilities: the motion could be **B**, **C** or **D**, and the two amendments

Table II.1 The threesome again

Preferences	Ms *i*	Mr *j*	Ms *k*
1st	A	B	C
2nd	B	C	D
3rd	C	D	A
4th	D	A	B

$$
\begin{array}{ccccccc}
B & & & & & & \\
\text{v} & = & B & & & & \\
C & & \text{v} & = & A & & \\
& & A & & \text{v} & = & D \\
& & & & D & &
\end{array}
$$

Fig. II.1 The first democratic debate—result

© The Editor(s) (if applicable) and The Author(s), under exclusive license to Springer Nature Switzerland AG 2022
P. Emerson, *The Punters' Guide to Democracy*,
https://doi.org/10.1007/978-3-031-06987-1

$$C$$
$$v \quad = \quad ....$$
$$D \qquad v \quad = \quad ....$$
$$B \qquad v \quad = \quad ....$$
$$A$$

Fig. II.2a Yet another democratic debate—procedure

$$C$$
$$v \quad = \quad C$$
$$D \qquad v \quad = \quad B$$
$$B \qquad v \quad = \quad A$$
$$A$$

Fig. II.2b Yet another democratic debate—result

C and *D*, *B* and *D* or *B* and *C* respectively. Let's start with the first setting, as in Fig. II.2a, which works out as Fig. II.2b, with the outcome now *A*.

A further democratic decision could be based on a status quo of *C*, a motion of *B* and amendments of *A* and *D*, in which case the threesome would want option *B*. And so on. With the above Table II.1's voters' profile, decision-making by binary vote is altogether a bit of a lottery. Again, so much depends on the order of voting as devised by the chair. The results of which-whatever way is chosen are in Table II.2.

In other words, for the four vegetables on the kitchen table, there are twelve different ways in which the subject could be tackled. And the answer could be anything, *A* or *B* or *C* or *D*, literally anything at all, yet always by a majority of 67%, with each and every outcome only *totally* democratic.

Table II.2 Permutations of manipulations

Status quo	Motion	The first binary ballot on the amendments	Preferred amendment	The second binary ballot	The sub-stantive	The third binary ballot, the final	The result
D	*A*	*B* and *C*	*B*	*A* or *B*?	*A*	*D* v *A*	*D*
D	*B*	*A* and *C*	*C*	*B* or *C*?	*B*	*D* v *B*	*B*
D	*C*	*A* and *B*	*A*	*C* or *A*?	*C*	*D* v *C*	*C*
A	*B*	*C* and *D*	*C*	*B* or *C*?	*B*	*A* v *B*	*A*
A	*C*	*B* and *D*	*B*	*C* or *B*?	*B*	*A* v *B*	*A*
A	*D*	*B* and *C*	*B*	*D* or *B*?	*B*	*A* v *B*	*A*
B	*A*	*C* and *D*	*C*	*A* or *C*?	*C*	*B* v *C*	*B*
B	*C*	*A* and *D*	*D*	*C* or *D*?	*C*	*B* v *C*	*B*
B	*D*	*A* and *C*	*C*	*D* or *C*?	*C*	*B* v *C*	*B*
C	*A*	*B* and *D*	*B*	*A* or *B*?	*A*	*C* v *A*	*C*
C	*B*	*A* and *D*	*D*	*B* or *D*?	*B*	*C* v *B*	*B*
C	*D*	*A* and *B*	*A*	*D* or *A*?	*D*	*C* v *D*	*C*

Annex III: The Single-peaked Curve

III.1 More Precision

When talking of cabbages and things, it is often quite difficult to put them into some sort of order. In a debate on tax rates, however, like the one we had in para 3.2.3, we can easily put them on a spectrum of high to low, and quite a few political disputes also cater for this sort of ordering: cheap to expensive, left-wing to right-wing, nationalist to internationalist, whatever.

So let's take that debate on tax rates again, and this time, with the list of five options: 40, 45, 50, 55 and 60%. If all concerned have decided to aim for a collective will to the nearest whole number, there are 21 different possible outcomes—any whole number from 40 to 60% inclusive: 40, 41, 42 … 60. And a ballot paper five-options long, allows for 120 different opinions or nuances to be expressed. But not all sets are logical.

III.1.2 Interpreting the Preferences

If my 1st preference is, say, 40%, my set of five preferences will be, logically,

$$40-45-50-55-60$$

© The Editor(s) (if applicable) and The Author(s), under exclusive
license to Springer Nature Switzerland AG 2022
P. Emerson, *The Punters' Guide to Democracy*,
https://doi.org/10.1007/978-3-031-06987-1

for points

$$5-4-3-2-1.$$

If however my 1st preference is 45%, a logical set of preferences could be either

$$45-40-50-55-60$$
$$45-50-40-55-60$$
$$45-50-55-40-60$$
or
$$45-50-55-60-40.$$

What I would probably not do is vote illogically, something like

$$45-55-40-60-50.$$

Converting the preferences into points—a 1st preference is 5, a 2nd 4, and so on—we could represent this last set of preferences in pictorial form, as in Graph III.1.

If I have cast just such a twin-peaked curve, then maybe I have tried either to vote tactically, or worse, to manipulate things... or worse again, I have been manipulated, (para 7.3, Footnote 7).

In contrast, a logical set of preferences will probably be seen as a single-peaked curve, as for example in Graph III.2 or Graph III.3.

And logically, there are 14 different sets of single-peaked preferences, as we shall see in Table III.2.

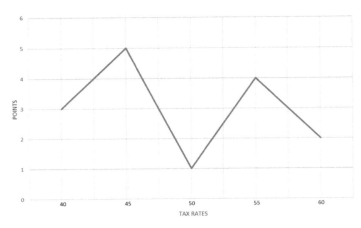

Graph III.1   A twin-peaked curve: 45–55–40–60–50

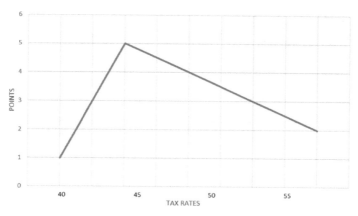

Graph III.2 A single-peaked curve: 45–50-55–60–40

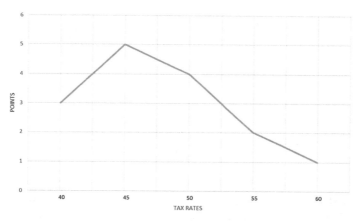

Graph III.3 Another single-peaked curve: 45–50–40–55–60

If the committee member has cast a logical set of preferences, his set of preferences will be single-peaked. Accordingly, in any debate where it is possible for the options to be listed in a logical spectrum, the set of preferences of every committee member will indicate whether or not she has voted logically or, to use the other word, sincerely.

And now comes an even nicer conclusion: if every member does indeed cast a full ballot of single-peaked preferences, the outcome, the collective set of preferences, will itself be single-peaked. Always. Take, for example, three voters: Ms i has preferences 45–50–55–60–40; Mr j opts for 55–50–45–60–40; and Ms k chooses 55–60–50–45–40.

We first translate these preferences into points, as shaded in Table III.1.

Table III.1   From Preferences to Points

		40	45	50	55	60
Ms i	preferences	5th	1st	2nd	3rd	4th
	points	1	5	4	3	2
Mr j	preferences	5th	3rd	2nd	1st	4th
	points	1	3	4	5	2
Ms k	preferences	5th	4th	3rd	1st	2nd
	points	1	2	3	5	4
	Points total:	3	10	11	13	8

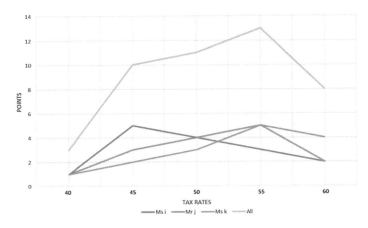

Graph III.4   The collective will

So for Ms i, Mr j and Ms k, that's 1–5–4–3–2, 1–3–4–5–2 and 1–2–3–5–4. We then collate these points, that is, add them up, as in the bottom row—3–10–11–13–8—and sure enough, this collective will is single-peaked, as in Graph III.4.

And if that collective single-peaked curve, as shown, peaks at 55% but leans moderately/heavily to the left, the Speaker shall conclude that, to the nearest whole number, the collective will is 53/54%. Exactly. The MBC is indeed a precision instrument.

III.2 Sets of Preferences

{In a binary contest between 40 and 60%, he who wants 53% (para 3.2.4) has to make a choice and vote tactically, while she who wants exactly 50% may be tempted to abstain.} In a preferential vote, the freedom of choice is greater, as in the following Table III.2, and the chair should publicise this precise interpretation of preferences, prior to the vote.

Table III.2　Precision preferences

The voter's aspiration	The voter's single-peaked set of preferences
40–42%	40–45–50–55–60
43–44%	45–40–50–55–60
45	45–50–40–55–60
46	45–50–55–60–40
47	50–45–40–55–60
48	50–45–55–40–60
49–51%	50–45–55–60–40
	50–55–45–40–60
52	50–55–45–60–40
53	50–55–60–45–40
54	55–50–45–40–60
55	55–50–45–60–40
56–57%	55–60–50–45–40
58–60%	60–55–50–45–40

So the voter can use this table, when choosing his set of preferences. The chair can use it too, as well as the collective single-peaked curve, when she interprets the results. Along with everything else in consensus politics, the process of compositing can also be completely transparent.

III.3 Choice

In a binary vote, the choice is just that, binary. In multi-option preferential ballots, however, there's a bit of pluralism. In a 3-option ballot, while there are those six ways of casting the preferences, (para 2.3.1), there are just four sets of single-peaked preferences, like this: assuming the 3 options—*A*, *B* and *C*—are in that order, the punter has a choice of a quartet of different single-peaked preference sets: the first starting with *A: A–B–C*; the fourth starting with *C: C–B–A*; and there are two in the middle starting with *B: B–A–C* and *B–C–A*.

In a 4-option ballot—and we'll assume the spectrum is now *A–B–C–D*—there are eight different sets of single-peaked preferences: *A–B–C–D* from one end; *D–C–B–A* from the other; three starting with *B, B–A–C–D, B–C–A–D* and *B–C–D–A*; and another threesome with *C* as the starting point, *C–D–B–A, C–B–D–A* and *C–B–A–D*.

Following the same logic, there are 14 different sets of preferences which may be expressed in a 5-option ballot, as in Table III.2. Precision makes perfect. While in a 6-option vote, with 720 different combinations of options possible, there is an even greater number of single-peaked preferences (it will take me a little time to work out the exact number, so here I'll just promise to put it into this book's second edition).

Annex IV: The Partial Vote

IV.1 Preference or Intransigence

Those who, for whatever reason, abstain from voting have no influence on the final decision. As we saw in para 2.4, those who submit a partial list of preferences in a modified Borda count MBC (quota Borda system QBS or matrix vote) have a partial influence. And of course, those who submit full ballots have a full influence.

So let's go back to Table 1.1 or Table 2.1, now repeated as Table IV.1, to see what happens in a partial vote, and we'll see that the difference between an MBC and a BC can be quite big.

As in para 2.2.7, the MBC social ranking of this voters' profile is

$$D\text{-}44, \; C\text{-}36, \; B\text{-}31, \; A\text{-}29, \qquad (\{\text{social ranking } (x)\})$$
$$D-C-B-A$$

Table IV.1 That same voters' profile

Preferences	Number of voters and their preferences			
	5	4	3	2
1st	A	B	C	D
2nd	D	D	D	C
3rd	C	C	B	B
4th	B	A	A	A

© The Editor(s) (if applicable) and The Author(s), under exclusive
license to Springer Nature Switzerland AG 2022
P. Emerson, *The Punters' Guide to Democracy*,
https://doi.org/10.1007/978-3-031-06987-1

Table IV.2 Another profile

Preferences	Number of voters and their preferences			
	5	4	3	2
1st	A	B	C	D
2nd	D	–	D	C
3rd	C	–	B	B
4th	B	–	A	A

and of course, with everyone submitting a full ballot, the result is the same with a BC. But what happens in a partial vote? Let's assume that all 4 of the **B** supporters decide that they don't trust this 'consensus nonsense' and opt to cast only a 1st preference; so the resulting profile is as seen in Table IV.2.

In a BC, {and we'll use rule (ii), $(n, n-1 \ldots 1)$ of (para 2.4)}, option **B** gets $4 \times 4 = 16$ points for its 1st preferences; but in an MBC it gets only $4 \times 1 = 4$ points.

The BC social ranking of Table IV.2 is

$$D\text{-}32, \textbf{\textit{B}}\text{-}31, \textbf{\textit{C}}\text{-}28, \textbf{\textit{A}}\text{-}25,$$
$$D-B-C-A$$

({social ranking (y)})

whereas the MBC social ranking is now

$$D\text{-}32, \textbf{\textit{C}}\text{-}28, \textbf{\textit{A}}\text{-}25, \textbf{\textit{B}}\text{-}19$$
$$D-C-A-B$$

({social ranking (z)})

In other words, as we said in para 2.4, the BC does not promote consensus. Quite the contrary—and in this respect it's rather like approval voting—a BC which allows partial voting under one of the n rules encourages the voters to be intransigent.

- When the **B** supporters all cast a full ballot, ({social ranking (x)}), **B** is third in the social ranking... and, as noted, with everyone casting full ballots, the BC and MBC social choices/rankings are identical.
- Submitting partial votes in a BC, however, ({social ranking (y)}), **B** is now in second place, and only one point behind the leader. In effect, therefore, the BC encourages people to truncate their votes, as M de Borda himself recognised (para 6.4).
- With an MBC count on Table IV.2, however, the difference works the other way: with full ballots, option **B** was ranked third overall, ({social ranking (x)}) but with partial ballots, **B** is now last, ({social ranking (z)}).

Table IV.3 For *B* or not for *B*

The count		Tables	Social ranking		*B*'s rank
Full ballots	BC/MBC	IV.1	(x)	*D–C–B–A*	Third
Partial ballots	BC	IV.2	(y)	*D–B–C–A*	Second
	MBC	IV.3	(z)	*D–C–A–B*	Fourth

The summary is shown in Table IV.3. In a nutshell, the MBC encourages all to participate… and to the full!

Obviously, potential winners will participate fully and need no persuasion. In a majoritarian democracy, as we have seen, minorities often abstain (or boycott, or turn to violence). In a consensual democracy, in contrast, everyone is better off if they are democratic. As was mentioned earlier, the MBC can identify the option with the highest *average* preference; and if folks want to influence that average, then they should indeed participate.

IV.2 Consensus Coefficients and Thresholds

When hundreds (in a parliament) or millions (in a referendum) participate in an MBC, the options' scores can be quite large and a bit unwieldly. So to make things simpler, we use a measure called a consensus coefficient, CC. For any one option, let's say option *A*, its CC_A is defined as option *A*'s MBC score, divided by what would have been the maximum possible score.

If we take the example of a committee of 12 members in a five-option ballot on options *A, B, C, D* and *E*, then the maximum score is a full dozen 1st preferences, which at 5 points each would give a score of 60. So if option *A* gets this maximum score, it gets the maximum CC, 60/60; and

$$CC_A = 1.00$$

If option *B* gets the minimum, a dozen 5th preferences, it gets a score of 12; so

$$CC_B = 12/60 = 0.2.$$

If option *C* gets the mean, a dozen 3rd preferences, it gets a score of $12 \times 3 = 36$; so

$$CC_C = 36/60 = 0.6.$$

If option D gets half a dozen 2nd preferences and half a dozen 4th, it gets a score of $(6 \times 4 + 6 \times 2) = 24 + 12 = 36$; so CC_D gets the same as CC_C:

$$CC_D = 36/60 = 0.6.$$

And lastly, if option E gets what's left, the other half dozen 2nd preferences plus half a dozen 4th, it too gets:

$$CC_E = 36/60 = 0.6.$$

In real life, what we normally do is suggest that, if the social choice option has a $CC \geq 0.9$, it represents the collective wisdom (para 3.3)—and its collective single-peaked curve, (Annex III), if there is one, will depict an alpine summit; if its ≥ 0.8, it's the consensus – and it's curve will show a more modest mountain; if ≥ 0.7, just the best possible compromise—a hill. And if it's only marginally above 0.6—if the curve is little more than an undulating plateau—then maybe it's better if the chair decides that there's no agreement at all and that no decision shall be taken; instead, as in the *barazas* of yesteryear, (para 6.2.1), the debate shall be resumed so that other options may be proposed, debated and then voted on.

IV.2.1 Consensus Coefficients Under Partial Voting

The above CC's apply, of course, only if everyone has submitted a full ballot. So now let us consider what happens if some people submit only partial ballots, and let's take another extreme case: a five-option ballot, in which no one votes for option E, at all. E therefore gets a score of 0 and $CC_E = 0.00$. {This of course is obviously a hypothetical case, because option E would not be on the ballot if someone(s) hadn't proposed it, and doubtless those who proposed would wish to give it a high if not indeed a 1st preference.} But if E does get a score of 0, then again, obviously, all of those voting for the other options will have cast only partial ballots. And if all 12 of the A supporters cast only four preferences, then the result of a dozen 1st preferences will give a score of only $12 \times 4 = 48$, so

$$CC_A = 0.8.$$

In effect, therefore, the CC of any one option is a measure, not only of that option's popularity, but also of the degree to which all concerned have participated in the democratic process. What it does not do is measure turnout; there again, as already mentioned (para 2.4), the MBC encourages everyone to participate and to the full, so ideally, this last measure is not so important—not, that is, in terms of the accuracy of the result.

IV.3 Aiming for Perfection

We can look at the imperfections of the Borda and Condorcet rules mathematically. The Condorcet rule, for example, can identify the option which wins all the pairings, but only if there is such a winner. When there's a paradox, we've got problems. So what we sometimes do is take the option which wins most of the pairings—the Copeland winner—which often solves the problem… but not always.

The MBC also has its weakness, as we mentioned in para 2.5: the problem of the irrelevant alternative. Basically, the elimination or addition of a (mathematically) irrelevant alternative can make a huge difference and on occasions change the resulting social choice and ranking.

Now in an election, no one candidate would like to be told that he or she is irrelevant, and all who are eligible and wishing to stand should indeed be allowed to do so. This is why it is sensible to have a procedure like (PR-STV or) QBS which actually encourages the party to nominate only as many candidates as it thinks it can get elected, so that every candidate is indeed relevant, politically, even if not mathematically.

Decision-making is a little more difficult, but as we saw in para 3.2.5, the MBC allows for compromise when the participants form the options, when the voters cast their preferences, and maybe too, in the analysis, when the chair forms a composite. So to cast a 2nd preference for what is in fact your last preference, as was suggested as a possible tactic in para 2.4.1, runs the risk that this last preference of yours will be composited into the final outcome. In other words, be careful what you vote for.

To a large extent, therefore, the procedures laid down for an MBC, allowing as they do the participants to form the options and then cast their full sets of preferences, and the chair to adjudicate perhaps on a composite, overcome the disadvantages associated with any irrelevant alternative, such that any complaints of this nature may themselves be seen as irrelevant.

Annex V: Consensus Coefficients

V.1 A Mean Average

In a ballot of five options, as we saw in para IV.2, the maximum consensus coefficient CC is 1.00, while the absolute minimum is 0.00. When everyone has cast a full ballot, the minimum CC is 0.2 and the mean CC is 0.6. With a different number of options, these values may vary, as in Table V.1.

V.2 The Thresholds

As a rough guide, we can also suggest some CC thresholds in order for the Speaker to classify the winning social choice into one of (not two, never

Table V.1 Consensus coefficients

Number of options	Absolute minimum	CC_{MIN}	CC_{MEAN}	CC_{MAX}
3	0.00	0.33	0.67	1.00
4		0.25	0.63	
5		0.20	0.60	
6		0.17	0.58	
7		0.14	0.57	
8		0.13	0.56	
9		0.11	0.55	
10		0.10	0.55	

P. Emerson, *The Punters' Guide to Democracy*, https://doi.org/10.1007/978-3-031-06987-1

Table V.2 The Thresholds

Number of options	CC_{MEAN}	No consensus	Best possible compromise	Consensus	Collective wisdom	CC_{MAX}
3	0.67	< 0.75	≥ 0.75	≥ 0.83		
4	0.63	< 0.72	≥ 0.72	≥ 0.81		
5	0.60	< 0.70	≥ 0.70	≥ 0.80	≥ 0.90	1.00
6	0.58	< 0.69	≥ 0.69	≥ 0.80		
7	0.57	< 0.68	≥ 0.68	≥ 0.80		
8	0.56	< 0.68	≥ 0.68	≥ 0.79		
9	0.55	< 0.67	≥ 0.67	≥ 0.79		
10	0.55	< 0.67	≥ 0.67	≥ 0.79		

two, but) three categories: best possible compromise, consensus and collective wisdom (para 3.3). But while the numbers in Table V.1 are all exact, the numbers shaded in Table V.2 should be regarded only as guidelines. As members of parliament become more used to working together, and more used to casting full ballots, so might the threshold levels be raised to the high levels shown here.

Annex VI: The Matrix Vote in Realpolitik

VI.1 The Completed Matrix Vote Ballot

An actual ballot paper, such as could be used in the *Bundestag*, the German Parliament, is shown in Table VI.1; it is designed for the fifteen cabinet posts which existed in September 2021, at the time of Germany's most recent election.

This particular example shows how a member of the Green Party GP might vote. She would know:

- that her party did not have enough support to compete for the post of Chancellor;
- that her top priority was for the environment ministry;
- that Robert Habeck and Annalena Baerbock were her party's top two priority nominees;
- that her party's most favoured partners would be members of the SPD and FDP;
- that because the matrix vote is PR, the relative strengths of the parties meant that the SPD, CDU, GP, FDP, AfD and Die Linke would probably get them 4+/4+/2/2/1/0 seats respectively in cabinet; and
- that she did not want to offer any support to the extreme right-wing AfD.

Accordingly, she might well have decided to give the GP her top three or even four preferences; and to cast her lower preferences for nominees from

© The Editor(s) (if applicable) and The Author(s), under exclusive license to Springer Nature Switzerland AG 2022
P. Emerson, *The Punters' Guide to Democracy*,
https://doi.org/10.1007/978-3-031-06987-1

Table VI.1   A completed matrix vote ballot

THE CABINET Names of candidates in order of preference		Chancellor	Finance	Interior	Foreign Affairs	Economy & Climate	Justice	Labour & Family	Defence	Food	Health	Digital & Transport	Environment	Education	Development	Special Tasks
Names	Party															
1ˢᵗ Robert Habeck	GP		B			A								C		
2ⁿᵈ Annalena Baerbock	GP			B	A		C									
3ʳᵈ Cem Özdemir	GP									A	C	B				
4ᵗʰ Anne Spiegel	GP							B	A						C	
5ᵗʰ Olaf Scholz	SPD	A														
6ᵗʰ Nancy Faeser	SPD			A												
7ᵗʰ Christine Lambrecht	SPD								A							
8ᵗʰ Christian Lindner	FDP		A													
9ᵗʰ Hubertus Heil	SPD														A	
10ᵗʰ Marco Buschmann	FDP						A									
11ᵗʰ Karl Lauterbach	SPD										A					
12ᵗʰ Ralph Brinkhaus	CDU													A		
13ᵗʰ Janine Wissler	DL												A			
14ᵗʰ Markus Söder	CDU													A		
15ᵗʰ Dorothy Bár	CDU															A

the other parties, as follows: the SPD 5, CDU 3, FDP 2, AfD 0 and DL 1. So her full ballot paper might well have been cast along the lines shown in Table VI.1.

NB The post-election government now consists of 17 members. Prior to the vote, all concerned would first agree as to the size of the future cabinet and specify its various ministries. In normal circumstances, the post-election cabinet would be the same as the previous one, and any changes in its size and structure would be for future consideration.

Annex VII: Emerson's Taxonomy of Decision-making

When voting on a decision, the extent to which the outcome can be described as representing the collective will, the consensus, (and the will of the majority), increases

(a) *as the voting procedure becomes more consensual and*
(b) *as the extent to which the number of options exceeds two... usually, on topics complex and/or controversial, up to a maximum of six.*

VII.1 Methodologies

Many voting procedures are used, supposedly, to identify the collective will of a set of voters—{not their unanimous viewpoint (which will be obvious and will not normally require a ballot)}—but their consensus, or maybe just their best possible compromise. The above taxonomy is based on an analysis of how decisions may be voted on, not only in elected/appointed chambers, committees and citizens' assemblies, but also in other settings such as referendums. The classification is based on the number of options on the ballot, the number of preferences a voter may cast, the number of those preferences that are counted, and the character of the procedure used for identifying the winning option.

© The Editor(s) (if applicable) and The Author(s), under exclusive license to Springer Nature Switzerland AG 2022
P. Emerson, *The Punters' Guide to Democracy*,
https://doi.org/10.1007/978-3-031-06987-1

VII.1.1 Binary Voting

In an adversarial (and at worst dictatorial) majority vote procedure, one powerful individual or group decides which question or which pair of options is to be voted on, and voters are faced with an "Option X, yes-or-no?" choice or, at best, an "Option X or option Y?" ballot. In many such votes, the phrasing of the question virtually determines the answer. In plebiscites, party caucuses and parliaments, the most obvious examples of dictatorial procedures were those binary votes taken by dictators, all trying to provide a veneer of legitimacy to their regimes. But this adversarial procedure is also used extensively in many parliamentary settings, where an individual or group, the executive, sets the agenda. In most instances, the authors of the question get the answer they want.

Political leaders in their national executives often have considerable powers as even the most complex problems are reduced to dichotomies—or series of dichotomies—with sequential parliamentary votes on amendments and the final substantive all taken on a 'for-or-against' basis. These votes are usually subject to a simple majority vote, but may be dependent on a weighted majority vote, and a minimum turnout or quorum may also be required. A less hierarchical methodology allows the people to propose the question, as in a Citizens' Initiative.

VII.1.2 Plurality Voting, Two-Round System, Serial Voting

In a multi-option non-preferential procedure, decisions are made from a choice of more than two options. The procedure may still be fundamentally majoritarian. The simplest of these is plurality voting, in which members of the given electorate may vote for one option only.

In a more complex, two-round system TRS, voters may vote for one of several options in the first round and, if no one option gains a majority, the two options with the highest totals are subject to a second-round majority vote.

In serial voting, a series of majority votes is taken between different pairs of options.

A few jurisdictions have used multi-option voting in referendums that offer from three to six or even seven options, using either plurality voting or a form of TRS to decide the winner.

VII.1.3 Modified Borda Count

A multi-option preferential procedure may enable decisions to be made from a list of more than two options by means of a non-majoritarian process. For example, the modified Borda count MBC, allows those concerned to participate, not only in voting on the final ballot, but also in choosing the options in the debate which precedes the ballot; this is sometimes delegated to elected representatives in parliament or selected individuals in a citizens' assembly.

With n alternatives, voters may cast m preferences, where $n \geq m \geq 1$, and m points are awarded to their 1st preference, $m-1$ to their 2nd preference, and so on. The outcome is the option with the highest total score.

VII.2 Analyses

VII.2.1 Binary Voting

Majority voting may be subject to a simple (50% + 1) or weighted majority (2/3rds or some other fraction greater than 1/2); to a double majority (sometimes used in Switzerland, when success depends upon a majority of the voters *and* a majority of the cantons); to a qualified majority (as in the European Union, so bigger countries like Germany have more clout than little ones like Malta); or to consociational majorities (as in Belgium or Cyprus, where the parliamentarians or electorate are divided into two constituencies and in which success depends on both majorities; in Bosnia in 1990, a three-way version was attempted... in vain).

VII.2.2 Multi-option Non-preferential Systems

There are five.

Plurality voting, in which voters cast only a 1st preference, and the option with the highest number of 1st preferences wins.

TRS is a plurality vote followed by a majority vote if no one option wins a majority in the first round.

In approval voting, the voter may 'approve' of more than one option, but each 'approval' has the same value—there are no preferences—and the option with the most 'approvals' wins.

Range voting gives the voter a fixed number of points that he/she can distribute to the various options at will: either some points to each of two or more options, or all the points to just one option.

Serial voting, in which, say, proposed amendments are listed in order, (cheap to expensive, or whatever); the procedure is a series of majority votes between the two extreme options, with the loser being eliminated after each vote; the outcome is perhaps a Condorcet winner (but see below).

VII.2.3 Multi-option Preferential Systems

There are four.

The alternative vote AV, (also known as instant run-off voting IRV, preference voting PV, ranked choice voting RCV and the single transferable vote STV), allows the voter to cast preferences for one, some or all the options listed. The count is a series of plurality votes, the least popular being eliminated after each stage and its votes transferred in accordance with its voters' 2nd and next highest preferences, until one option gains majority support.

The Borda count BC asks the voters to cast their preferences, and points are awarded to (1 , 2 ... last) preferences cast according to the rule (n, $n-1$ ... 1) or ($n-1$, $n-2$ ... 0); this procedure may encourage the voters to truncate their vote.

The modified Borda count MBC allows for partial voting. It uses M de Borda's original formula, (m, $m-1$ ... 1), and this encourages the voters to cast a preference for every option.

The Condorcet rule compares the preferences cast for each option in pairings. The option which wins the most pairings and therefore beats every other option—if there is such a victor—is the Condorcet winner. If there isn't one, the option which wins the most pairings is chosen, (the Copeland rule). There may, however, be a paradox.

The MBC and Condorcet are the only methodologies which always take all preferences cast by all voters into account; not least for this reason, they can be claimed to be the most inclusive and therefore most consensual procedures, and to provide the most accurate measure of the will of the said set of voters. Indeed, in many voters' profiles, the MBC social choice is also the same as the Condorcet social choice, and even the social rankings are often similar.

Table VII.1 Decision-making systems—a comparison

Preferences counted	BINARY		MULTI-OPTION NON-PREFERENTIAL		MULTI-OPTION PREFERENTIAL
all					MBC
					Condorcet
lots					BC
some			Approval voting		
			Range voting		
a few			TRS	Serial voting	AV/IRV/PV/RCV/STV
1st only	Weighted majority	Consoc-iational			
	Simple majority	Double majority	Plurality voting		
	one		some		one, some or all
	1 of 2 options		1 of some options	1 or some of all options	1 or some or all of all options
	Preferences cast				

VII.3 Voting Procedures in Decision-Making

Voting procedures used in decision-making vary from the exclusive and blunt binary ballot in the bottom left-hand corner of Table VII.1, to the inclusive and accurate MBC in the top-right corner.

NB Colour-coding is from red (least consensual) to green (most consensual).

Range voting allows the voters to be consensual, but incentivises them to be the very opposite; hence the grey.

Glossary

Absolute majority	50% +1 or more.
Alternative vote AV	A decision-making or an electoral system. In a ballot of n options (candidates), a voter may cast preferences —1, 2, 3...—as many as he likes. AV is a majoritarian knock-out system. At each stage of the count, if no one option has a majority, the least popular option is eliminated and its votes are transferred in accordance with its voters' 2nd (or subsequent) preferences. The process continues until an option gains more than 50%; (paras 2.2.3 and 5.2.5). AV is the same as IRV, PV, RCV and STV. It can be used as an electoral system in single-member constituencies, as in Australia, or in its PR format in multi-member constituencies, as in Ireland. See also monotonicity.
Approval voting	This decision-making or electoral system is non-preferential. A voter may support as many options (candidates) as she wishes, but each 'approval' has the same value, (para 2.2.5).

P. Emerson, *The Punters' Guide to Democracy*, https://doi.org/10.1007/978-3-031-06987-1

Binary voting	This system is usually associated with decision-making. The voter has a choice of only two options—"*A* or *B?*"—or maybe it's a choice on just one option—"*A*, yes or no?"
Borda count BC	Similar to the MBC, the BC can be used in decision-making and in elections. In a BC, points are awarded according to the rule *(n, n–1 ... 1)* or *(n–1, n–2 ... 0)*; (para 2.4).
Citizens' assembly	A decision-making forum in which the participants—a fixed number of about 100 or so citizens—are chosen by lot. Its decisions are usually non-binding recommendations, the final decision to be taken later either in parliament or in a referendum.
Citizens' initiative	When a vote is called for by a certain large number of citizens in any jurisdiction which caters for a citizens' initiative, the government must hold the requisite referendum.
Clone	An option which is almost the same as another option.
Coalition	A political party is the coming together of various persons, prior to an election; a coalition—majority, grand or all-party—is what might happen afterwards.
Common good	The greatest good for the greatest number.
Composite	The amalgamation of two options into one.
Condorcet	A preferential decision-making or electoral voting system which aims to identify the option (candidate) which wins the most pairings, (para 2.2.8). (See also Copeland.)
Consensus	Consensus is not unanimity. Rather, a consensus opinion is one on which perhaps (almost) all concerned are agreed to compromise.

Consensus coefficient, CC	The consensus coefficient CC of option A, CC_A, is option A's MBC score divided by the maximum possible score which option A could have achieved, if every voter had given A their 1st preference. Accordingly, a CC may vary from 0.00 which is minimal to 1.00 which is the maximum, (para 2.2).
Consociationalism	Some pluralist societies require twin majorities, and if a majority of 'these' people *and* a majority of 'those' both say 'yes', then 'yes' it is.
Copeland	In a Condorcet count, if no one option wins all the pairings to become the Condorcet winner, a Copeland winner (if one exists) is the option (or candidate) which wins the most pairings.
Filibuster	A speech which goes on and on until the debate runs out of time.
First-past-the-post, FPTP	This electoral system is like a plurality vote; (para 5.2.2).
Free vote	A vote is deemed to be free when individual members are able to vote according to their conscience and/or their constituents' wishes, rather than in line with any instructions from a party whip.
Full ballot	In an MBC ballot of n options (candidates), a voter is said to have submitted a full ballot if she has cast a valid preference to all n options (candidates). When $n > 10$, it might be decided that a full ballot shall be a fixed number of, say, 6 preferences. (See also partial ballot.)
Impossibility theorem	Kenneth Arrow's theorem suggests that no voting procedure can be perfect, immune

	from irrelevant alternatives, paradoxes and certain other criteria (Sect. 6.4.1).
Irrelevant alternative	An option, often less popular than an existing option, the addition or subtraction of which can change the MBC social choice and ranking.
Matrix vote	This electoral voting procedure can be used when a certain number of individuals elect a team, a specific number of officer holders, each with a different function. The voters have the ability to choose, in order of preference, not only those whom they wish to be an office holder, but also the office in which they wish each nominee to serve (Chap. 4).
Modified Borda count MBC	The MBC is designed for decision-making (para 2.2.7), but it can also be used as an electoral system, (para 2.2.10). In a ballot of n options (or candidates), a voter may cast m preferences, so obviously,
	$n \geq m \geq 1$
	Points are awarded to (1st, 2nd ... last) preferences cast according to the rule
	$(m, m{-}1 \ldots 1)$
	See para 2.4.
	The MBC is not proportional; see QBS.
Monotonicity	If an option becomes more popular and gets a higher score, it should have a greater chance of winning. If however the voting procedure is not monotonic, it might actually have less chance! Umm, sounds odd. Let's take an example, which starts with Table G.1, 23 voters with preferences as shown.

Table G.1   Monotonicity: the First Ballot

8	2	4	3	6
A	A	B	B	C
B	C	A	C	B
C	B	C	A	A

Table G.2   Monotonicity: the Second Ballot

8	4	3	2	6
A	B	B	C	C
B	A	C	A	B
C	C	A	B	A

So **A** has 10 1st preferences, **B** has 7, and **C** has 6. In an AV stage (i) count, **C** is eliminated, its 6 votes go to **B**, so **B** gets a score of 13 compared to **A**'s 10, and **B** wins.

But what happens if the 2 voters in the shaded column vote, not **A–C–B**, but **C–A–B?** So **C** has become more popular, **A** less popular, and **B** is the same. We move to Table G.2.

This gives a stage (i) score line of **A**-8, **B**-7, **C**-8, so **B** is now eliminated. 4 of its votes go to **A** and 3 go to **C**, to give a stage (ii) score of **A**-12 and **C**-11, so the winner is now option **A**. Good heavens: when 2 voters go from **A-C-B** to **C-A-B**, in other words, when option **A** becomes less popular in the vote, it becomes more popular in the count! That should be impossible, but if a voting procedure is not monotonic, like AV and PR-STV, anything might happen! {This is an adaptation of the example given in (Dummett 1997: 101), referenced in Chap. 7}.

Multi-member constituency	In an FPTP election, a single-member constituency elects just one person. With PR, it's more than one in a multi-member constituency.
	If 2 are to be elected, well, that's not very proportional, and not much good for any parties with less than a quota of 33% support. So multi-member constituencies often elect 3–6 members, but if the entire country is one multi-member constituency, like the Netherlands, then the one constituency elects all 150 members of the parliament, and the Dutch quota is 0.7%, (para 5.2).
Multi-member proportional MMP	This electoral system gives the voter two ballot papers: the first is for an FPTP election in a small, local constituency; the second is for a PR-list election in a much larger, regional ornational, constituency. MMP is used in Germany and New Zealand, (para 5.2.11).
Paradox	If one person has (1st-2nd-3rd) preferences A-B-C, a second person ranks them as B-C-A, and a third opts for C-A-B, the pairings are A > B, B > C and C > A, which means that A > B > C > A ....and it goes round and round for ever. It is called the 'paradox of binary voting', (para 1.3).
Parallel voting	Like MMP, this is a two-tier electoral system of FPTP (or TRS) plus PR-list, the difference being that in MMP, the overall result is proportional, whereas in parallel voting, only the second PR bit is proportional, and sometimes this bit is not very big. In Taiwan and

	Japan, it's about 37%, in Pakistan, a mere 20%.
Partial ballot	In an MBC on n options, if a voter submits only m preferences, where $m < n$, he is said to submit a partial ballot, as in Annex IV.
Party structure	Systems of governance which vary from the one-party state, via two-party and multi-party to an all-party coalition or government of national unity GNU, (which maybe completes the circle).
Plebiscite	See referendum.
Plurality vote	In this decision-making system, a ballot of n options, a voter may cast only one preference. The winner is the option with the most votes cast in its favour; it may be a majority, or maybe just the largest minority, (para 2.2.1).
Preference voting, PV	See AV.
Preferendum	A multi-option referendum can be analysed in a number of different ways. The MBC is a Borda preferendum.
PR-list	In this type of electoral system, each party displays a list of its candidates. In a closed list system, the voter may choose one party only. Most open systems allow the voter to choose one candidate from the party of their choice, (but see para 5.2.8).
Profile, voters'	An anonymous table showing the number of preferences cast for all the options.
Proportional representation, PR	There are several PR electoral systems, from PR-list closed and open to PR-STV and QBS.
PR-STV	This is an AV or STV election conducted in multi-member constituencies. Candidates with a quota of 1st preferences get elected; their surplus votes are re-distributed as

	are those of any least popular candidates, until the required number of candidates has reached the quota, (para 5.2.9). See also monotonicity.
Ranked choice voting, RCV	See AV.
Quota	In a vote on only two options, the winner is that which gains 50% + 1 of the vote. With three options, success might need only 33% + 1. With four options, the quota as it is called is about 25% + 1, (para 5.2.2).
Quota Borda system, QBS	A PR electoral system based on an MBC: the voter casts her preferences, and a candidate's success depends on either a good number of top preferences and/or a good MBC score, (para 5.2.12).
Range voting	A decision-making system in which each voter is given, say, 6 or 10 points, and these she can allocate as she wishes, either all to just one favourite, or various small sums to a few options; (para 2.2.6).
Referendum	A decision-making vote for the entire electorate. Binding or non-binding, it is usually binary but can be multi-optional.
Relative majority	The term rather contradicts itself: in a plurality vote, if the option which gets the most has >50%, it is said to have an absolute majority; if it is <50%, it is said to have a relative majority… which actually is only the largest minority.
Right of majority rule	No majority has the right to dominate, and no minority the right to veto. All share a responsibility to seek the common good.
Right of self-determination	The right of a people—whatever that is—to define their own nation and its system of governance.
Serial voting	A knock-out system of decision-making, a series of majority votes on a spectrum of options, (para 2.2.4).

Sincere voting	A voter who casts her preferences as they really are, is said to vote sincerely. As opposed to tactical voting.
Single-peaked curve	If the options on a ballot paper may be ordered in a spectrum, and if a voter's preferences (on the y-axis) when displayed against these options (on the x-axis) indicate the voter's decreasing enthusiasm for these options, to one side and/or the other, of her 1st preference, her set of preferences are said to be single-peaked.
Single transferable vote, STV	See AV.
Social choice	The option which society wants most of all.
Social ranking	The social choice of every option, in order of popularity.
Tactical voting	The opposite of sincere voting. A voter may cast a 2nd and subsequent preferences, not as he would wish, not as he would in sincere voting, but for a tactical purpose, in an effort either to maximise advantage for his own favourite, or to decrease the chances of an option he strongly opposes.
Two-round system, TRS	This decision-making or electoral system consists of a plurality vote followed, if nothing gains a majority, by a majority vote between the two leading options, (para 2.2.2).
Two-tier voting system	An election may involve two votes, one in small constituencies, the second in larger areas. The former is usually FPTP, TRS or PR-list election; the latter is invariably a PR-list election.
Veto	The so-called right of veto gives the holder the ability to override the democratic choice of everybody else. (See right of majority rule.)

Whip

A party whip (animate noun) may whip (verb) his party members to do as he demands; those who disobey may lose the whip (inanimate noun).

Index